31 DAYS OF **HOPE**
Reinvented

By: Denise Pass

www.denisepass.com

Copyright © 2017 by Denise Pass
All rights reserved. This book or any portion thereof may not be reproduced or used in any manner whatsoever without the express written permission of the publisher except for the use of brief quotations in a book review or scholarly journal.

First Printing: 2016
ISBN 9781387010769

Seeing Deep Ministries
P.O. Box 1262
Locust Grove, VA

www.denisepass.com

HOPE REINVENTED

31 Day Devotional

Psalm 147:11

"The Lord delights in those who fear him, who put their hope in his unfailing love."

(C) 2016 Denise Pass.
All rights reserved.

I dedicate this book first and foremost to God, my Deliverer; the One Who has restored my hope and is the lifter of my head. He has made beauty from ashes and used what I never would have wanted to happen and turned it into a testimony of His amazing grace and enablement.

Our God is always faithful, friends. He will never abandon or forsake us and His ways are truly good all the time.

Secondly, I dedicate this book to you. No matter what this life has brought to you, God passionately cares about you and is pursuing you this very moment. Don't give up trusting in Him. Lay down your hope and adopt His, instead.

Finally, I dedicate this book to my precious family who endured the early mornings and late evenings while I wept and wrote lovingly this book. This work has been a calling that I could not get away from, urged on in the Spirit to write, it sometimes meant sacrificing time. My family surrounded me in this effort and this work would not have been written if they had not. I love you, my precious husband and children.

31 Days of Hope Reinvented
Day 1: Salvation is Here

Inspirational Thought of the Day:
Hope would be meaningless if we did not have a living God Who makes and fulfills His promises.

Scripture of the Day: *1 Peter 1:3-6*
*"Blessed be the God and Father of our Lord Jesus Christ! By his great mercy he gave us new birth into a **living hope** through the resurrection of Jesus Christ from the dead, that is, into an inheritance imperishable, undefiled, and unfading. It is reserved in heaven for you, who by God's power are protected through **faith for a salvation** ready to be revealed in the last time."*

Ever feel like salvation looks a little different than what you had hoped for? I mean, if we are on the Jesus team now, life should be unicorns and roses without the thorns, right? Or maybe you haven't accepted the free gift of salvation yet because you are not sure you can hope in one more thing that will possibly let you down. Seriously, life can send us some hard times and it is not enough to quote some nice sounding sayings to get us through it all.

Our hope in God can begin to falter when we pray and we pray and circumstances don't change. Where is God when life hurts? Why doesn't He choose to end our pain sometimes?

It seems wrong to question, but in all honesty, *the only path to healing and finding genuine hope is to walk through the door of pain and seek to understand the heart of God in it all.*

It is in the moment of our angst and grief that we find more than comfort in God's Word and His presence. We discover a purpose and a hope far less superficial than the quest for a perfectly pain-free life, and God surprises us with a living hope in Him.

If you have ever wondered where God was when you discovered the most horrific, painful truth that shattered your life and family, or your home was foreclosed, or when you suffer with multiple illnesses, or your marriage ends in divorce or your pregnancy ends in miscarriage .. the list goes on and on with the disappointments life can bring... you are not alone.

I've wondered, too, when I walked through all of the things I just mentioned. But that wondering has been transformed into a wonder at how awesome God is – even when life hurts.

Religiously saying He is there or won't give us more than we can handle doesn't cut it when the sky is falling. He is not just there when we suffer – He **chose** the suffering we seek to avoid – because He loves us so much. When He chose to be rejected by men, spat upon and to bear our punishment, the Bible says He had joy. He endured His suffering knowing firmly the hope He had. In His immense suffering, He knew what He was accomplishing in that suffering – the salvation of many.

So it is with us. When we suffer and long for our deliverance, long for just a glimmer of hope again, God is accomplishing something far greater than granting relief from our temporary pain. He is **changing our hope** and making us into His image, in addition, He is also giving us grace in our time of need.

To be human is to hope – to hope and believe in an ultimate good end. God uniquely made us with a craving for hope and something more than we see around us. *This is not ingratitude, but a longing placed there by a sovereign God, who knew we needed to be people of Hope to live worthy lives.*

He does not tell us to hope and then crush our dreams. *Hope would be meaningless if we did not have a living God Who makes and fulfills His promises.* Hope is an overused word that can lose its meaning unless we begin to look deeper into what this hope really is like that God has for us.

The Scripture reference says that when we are saved, we are saved into a living hope. Not just a concept, nor a thing to strive for – this hope is alive and given to us. Our hope is alive because our Savior is alive. This does not mean the removal of pain or sorrow, but it does mean He will rescue us. It might be a mighty deliverance that brings Him glory or it might mean an awesome testimony of His enablement throughout. The irony of God's salvation is that God does not always save us **from** our troubles, but He often saves us **through** our troubles.

Some of the most amazing men of God in the Bible died, never having seen their hope fulfilled, yet their hope was certain.

Their hope was beyond the grave and eternal.

When we feel without hope, it is in that moment that our hope is in the wrong place. Don't get me wrong – it is not wrong to hope to see the goodness of God in the land of the living – the Psalmist echoed the same heart cry – but when our hope is in Him alone, we are no longer disappointed.

There is an awe that God will somehow use the mess to bless and also glorify Himself. He promises to. Instead of hoping I will no longer have to suffer, I now hope that I can honor God in every situation that arises.

During one of the greatest sorrows of my life, I was crying out to God and asking Him why He let someone else's sins destroy my life and why I was suffering consequences for their sins. "I wasn't angry when I bore your sins" was the answer. God forgive me. I had forgotten about His glory and felt forgotten by my loving Father, when He was inviting me to get hope and strength from Him in the midst of the fire.

On the day God drew me to Himself, I was saved from eternal suffering, but my circumstances did not change. I was submerged into a deluge of newfound persecution, but my heart was full of hope. This is the mystery of a supernatural hope – it does not depend on anything this world has, but is firmly anchored in God alone.
This hope is anchored in a future salvation that is yet to be fully revealed. It is not anchored in a problem-free, perfect life on earth.

As we explore this hope together, 1 Peter 1:3-6 reminds us that this salvation is a **living hope**. Our salvation is a constant hope that we look to and can depend on. It never fades, it is certain. It is a relationship with the God Who made us.

One last promise to keep us going – Jesus is interceding for us. He knows we get discouraged. He will not fail us and will restore our hope if we will just hang on to His word and promises.

A Time to Worship

The song, _In Christ Alone by the Gettys_ reminds us where our hope truly is - only in His righteousness; only in Jesus.

Hebrews 7:25: "Therefore he is able to save completely those who come to God through him, because he always lives to intercede for them."

Inspirational Thought of the Day:
Hope is fragile if it is dependent on a perfect life. The strength of a hope in Christ is that we hope beyond what we are feeling.

Scripture of the Day: *2 Corinthians 1:8-11*
"We do not want you to be uninformed, brothers and sisters, about the troubles we experienced in the province of Asia. We were under great pressure, far beyond our ability to endure, so that we despaired of life itself. Indeed, we felt we had received the sentence of death. But this happened that we might not rely on ourselves but on God, who raises the dead. He has delivered us from such a deadly peril, and he will deliver us again. On him we have set our hope that he will continue to deliver us, as you help us by your prayers. Then many will give thanks on our behalf for the gracious favor granted us in answer to the prayers of many."

Hoping is easier when all is well. But when it seems the ground beneath you has not just been shaken, but has disappeared altogether, where is the Christian to stand? On higher ground.

At first this higher ground is on our knees, desperate for understanding and compassion from our God. With no fight left, surrender to God might seem easy, but depression or fear try to keep us from hoping at all.

Maybe we quote some verses or sing a song to try to help pull ourselves up in our new reality. Maybe we get angry, or cry or call friends – anyone who can offer a tonic to numb our pain. Maybe we stare blankly at the walls around us, pinching ourselves to see if we are awake.

We can't go back to the place we were before the pain entered our lives. We can't move forward, either. Daily functioning becomes an exercise in futility and feels like walking in mud. Our hearts are gripped with shock and horror that threatens to paralyze any movement at all.

A crisis happens when we encounter this moment when life simply hurts. We grasp for any sense of "normalcy", whatever that is, and secretly in our hearts can begin to question God's love and goodness.

Ever felt this kind of hopelessness? Sorry if I paint a grim picture. We have to be real and honest – in order to see our need for a hope that is tenacious in the face of suffering.

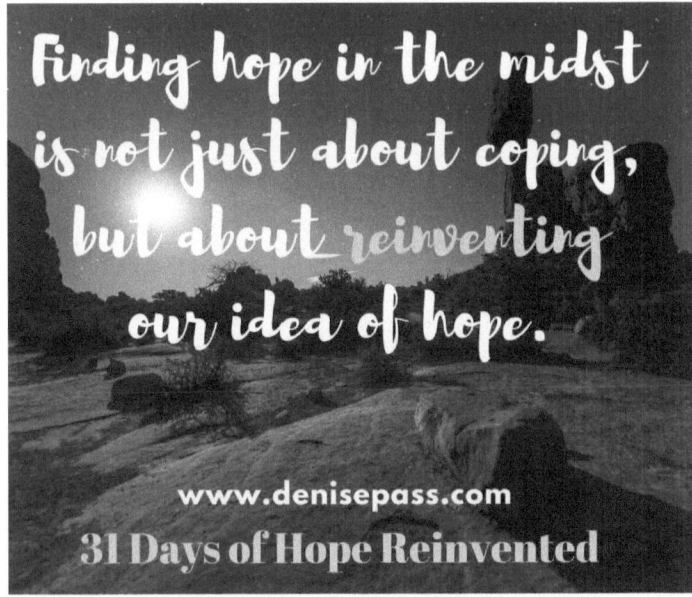

The day God revealed to me the sin of the father of my children I could not breathe. The shame, horror and complete shock enveloped me. I did what any sensible woman would do. I ate chocolate. A lot of it. Buffalo wings, too. I spent over our budget just to try to bring joy to my children. I wept and wept some more. I cried out for understanding and suffered shunning and a new social status that threatened to steal my joy. How did I get there?

This was not supposed to happen. I had waited for marriage and married a Christian man. I had promised to protect my children. In a state of grief, I could not feel my hands or feet and was dragged to court incessantly by the one who inflicted on us all our pain. Trying to homeschool five children while being falsely accused was a mess. But still I had this thing inside of me – what was it? Hope.

Hope that the God who promised to use everything for my good and His glory would do so. Hope that my God <u>saw</u> <u>me</u>. On the witness stand. On the floor, crying out for His deliverance. I read His Scripture night and day, trying to find answers that would help me to hold on just one more day. *This hope was a constant anchor that I had to cultivate in God's word.*

If you have never gone through something traumatic that has rocked your world, hang tight. This world does not promise a perfect life. If you have suffered something that has left you disillusioned, you are in the right place.

Suffering is common to man. There are lots of books on the subject, but having genuine joy, hope and victory when the trials **continue** is uncommon. Finding hope in the midst is not just about coping, but about **reinventing our idea of hope** and navigating disillusionment to find real hope in God's sovereignty, promises and character rather than in our circumstances.

So how do we let go of Kansas?

                      It may have been all we ever knew.

The grief process of letting go of our perception of what we thought our life in Christ should have looked like is not easy; but it is a well worn path by many who can testify of God's miracles reaching into their circumstances and transforming their heart and hope in the midst.

It is not until we are submerged in the most challenging trials of our lives that we realize where our hope is placed.

The former hope was based conceptually, this new hope experientially. The former hope was developed when we were surrounded by blessing, this new hope was developed in brokenness and is no longer dependent upon circumstances.

Our innocence gone, our hope in the happy fairy tale ending smashed to pieces on the floor, we have to find a new hope that is not manufactured by rote, but rather fashioned in the fire. Tough questions need to be asked to find hope again. Authentic questions that pour out our heart before God. At this place of raw suffering and crying out to God we present an honest offering – a sacrifice of praise, that becomes an internal hope that cannot be put out.

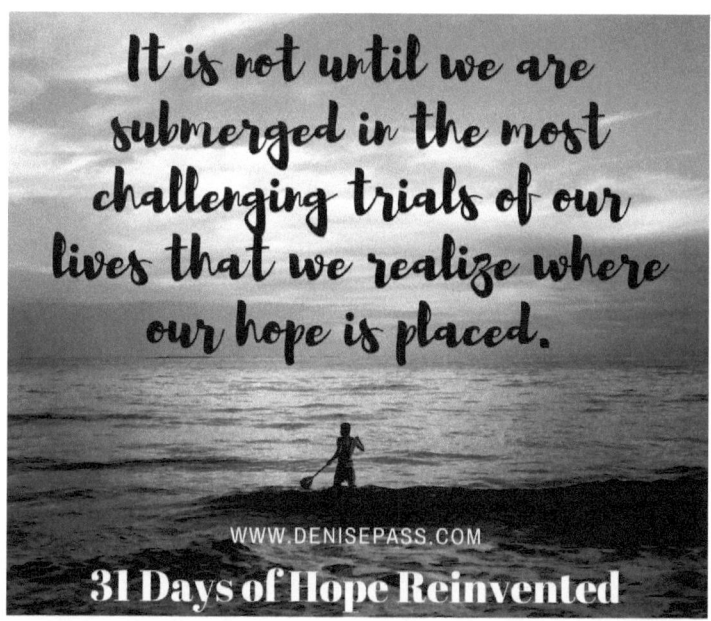

Paul understands. He wanted everyone to know the fire he had passed through – not to be a whiner, but to be real and to give God the glory. He shared his secret, too. He found his hope in relying on the One Who rose from the dead. Anyone Who can do that can handle our problems.

While we are not in our Kansas anymore, the new place we are at is deep. Deep in Christ. We understand His suffering. We understand that He left Heaven to come and suffer for us. He understands what it is like to leave perfection behind for those He loves. He left Heaven and we had to leave our Kansas.

We cannot get back what we thought we owned, but when we see the amazing treasures God gives us while we process trauma, we would not want to go back there, anyway. In its place is now a genuine desire and acceptance of what God has for us, which far surpasses our former hopes and dreams.

Hope is fragile if it is dependent on a perfect life. The strength of a hope in Christ is that we hope beyond what we are feeling.

A Time to Worship

Supernaturally, God enables us to hope when it seems ludicrous to do so. Recently, I had the joy of thanking Sara Groves for a song she wrote that embodied what I felt during this season of searching for hope in my life. I thought you might enjoy it, too – <u>Painting Pictures of Egypt.</u>

Lord, I pray for each one reading this blog – that you would fill them with your inexpressible hope and give them Your promises whispered to their heart. You are forever faithful and we worship You!

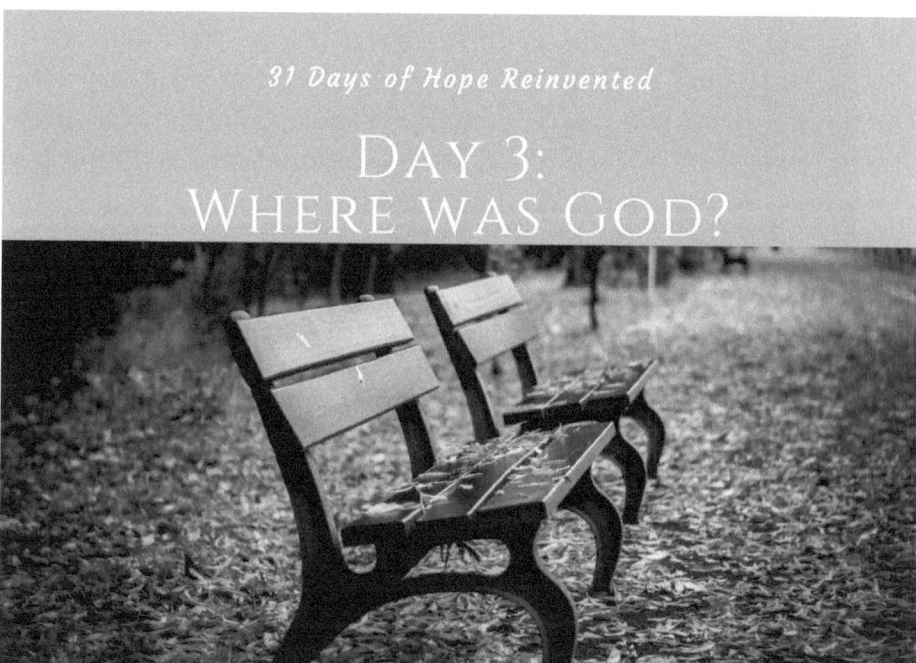

Inspirational Thought of the Day:
When we are wounded by life's uncertainty, God loves to be our hero who uses the pain to wreck our religiosity and cause our hard hearts to become soft again.

Scripture of the Day: *Hebrews 6:15-19*
15 "And so by persevering, Abraham inherited the promise. 16 For people swear by something greater than themselves, and the oath serves as a confirmation to end all dispute. 17 In the same way God wanted to demonstrate more clearly to the heirs of the promise that his purpose was unchangeable, and so he <u>intervened with an oath</u>, 18 so that we who have found refuge in him may find <u>strong</u> encouragement to <u>hold fast to the hope set before</u> us through two unchangeable things, since it is impossible for God to lie. 19 <u>We have this hope as an anchor for the soul</u>, sure and steadfast, which reaches inside behind the curtain, where Jesus our forerunner entered on our behalf, since he became a priest forever in the order of Melchizedek."

In the midst of the biggest heartaches of our lives, our faith in God is under siege. Voices around us and inside our own heart betray us and beg us to accuse God for the calamity that has come upon us.

Given everything we have, still we feel we have a right to it all. In His sovereign wisdom, God created us without the ability of being able to control anything and with no certain promises in this world except Himself. We all want to be able to count on something in this life and it is sometimes frightening when we cannot.

This human condition of dependency causes us to engage in many futile efforts of trying to overcome our dependent status. We can begin attempting to control our life or others, becoming angry with God, people or circumstances that we cannot control, or maybe at the end of ourselves, we bring our hurt to the only One Who can heal us – the One Who designed us to be in relationship with Himself.

Our genius God who made us to depend on Him did not do it with any other motive than love. Our hearts drift away – that is the norm. And when life is hard, our hope begins to fade, too. So where was God when we suffered our biggest sorrow, illness, financial woe? I know, I know. If I say "he was there", that is hard to understand. If He was there, why didn't He stop it?

This question has caused many to doubt God's goodness and yet *the very same part of us who craves independence from God wants dependence if it means He can fix all of our problems.* A little hypocritical, perhaps.

God is not insecure. He does not need us, but He loves us so much that He gave His own life for ours and lets us choose how we will live. He gives us a free will and although he is in complete control of the universe, we have the ability to choose sin or obedience. Death or life. There are consequences for those choices and when we or other people in our lives choose sin, we will be impacted. Is God to blame for that?

In the darkest moments of my searching for God in our mess, the LORD showed me that there were many layers in my heart. Layers of hurt, doubt, unbelief. I said I believed in God. But there were layers tucked beneath that could not fully trust the God Who could allow such pain in.

When we are wounded by life's uncertainty, God loves to be our hero who uses the pain to wreck our religiosity and cause our hard hearts to become soft again.

I did not want my faith hurt or my children's faith hurt from the actions of their father. The fact that he professed to be a Christian made our trauma even worse. In that place of desperation for healing and crying out to God that He would help me to raise my children and keep their hearts and faith strong, the LORD amazed me.

He did not remove my problems but He did change our hearts. Over and over again His promises stood out. They were not just nice sounding, fluffy wishes. They were real. They were for us. And they were accessed by His Holy Spirit, revealing the truth and helping us to believe and hold on to each precious promise.

"I would have despaired if I had not believed I would see the goodness of God in the land of the living." Those words from the Psalmist cut my heart wide open. Oh, God. I want to believe that my life will not always be a heap of ruins. God can do a lot with a willing heart who asks for help to believe when everything seems hopeless.

If someone has hurt you seemingly irreparably, know this: God is for you. He does not change, He is incapable of lying. Every single one of His promises are for you, if you will just persevere.

I can hear some saying impatiently, "I need that promise now". So do I, friend. So do I. But when we begin to trust His promises He also reveals our need to trust Him with what is best for us. What we consider mercy might not be mercy. What we consider blessing might lead us to a curse. Father knows best. He is our Promise Maker & Promise Keeper and His ways are perfect.

As we move on toward maturity in Christ, we are no longer like little children who need to be given what we demand in order to feel loved. Instead, we stand in awe at the character of our God – unfailing, perfect in every way, and the fact that He would offer us promises at all – the ones who violated His perfect law – and we can only worship with gratitude.

Surrendering our hearts to Him and asking Him to help us trust Him when we don't understand – is complete freedom. He is able to enable us when life is hard and turn our ashes into a thing of beauty.

A Time to Worship

I wrote the song, *Layers* last year out of this testimony of surrender that God led me through. I pray it encourages you, today, as well. Peel back the Layers of your heart and lay them at His feet. Expose and surrender the hurt and fears before the One Who wipes away every one of our tears.

Oh, Lord! You are so beautiful, so faithful, so good! Thank You for Your precious promises. Help us to cling to You and to Your promises and to never grow weary in doing so.

Inspirational Thought of the Day:
The secret of the desert is to not look at all the pain around us, but to look to the One Who made the desert.

Scriptures of the Day:
Job 17:15
"Where then is my hope – who can see any hope for me?"

Isaiah 35:1
"Let the desert and dry region be happy; let the wilderness rejoice and bloom like a lily!"

Isaiah 43:19
"Look, I am about to do something new...Do you not recognize it? Yes, I will make a road in the desert and paths in the wilderness."

Hosea 13:5
"I took care of you in the wilderness, in that dry and thirsty land."

The desert is a beautiful place if we have eyes to see it. Some just see the dust and the dearth of anything green and lush. There seems to be no life there.

Some fear the scary critters lurking and slithering all around. Others see the majestic mountains in the backdrop, and the brave life that sneaks up through the cracks in the ground, bursting forth with promise.

I grew up out west and New Mexico left a big impact on me. Or maybe on my derrière. I recall vividly walking on top of a fence (because this is what sensible people do) and falling to my demise right on top of a cactus. The hours spent having someone else pull needles out of my bum taught me a lesson that I have not forgotten – the desert hurts.

The scorpions and tarantulas added to my distaste of the desert, too. Walking home from school with the mighty March winds stinging my legs while dodging flying tumbleweeds, I confess that while the terrain was beautiful in this desert, it was harsh, too.

God's people knew the desert well – they spent a lot of time there. They did not appreciate it and complained about God's provision while they were there.They remembered the provision they had while enslaved and favored that place of shame and suffering instead of being dependent upon God in a dry season. Not a lot has changed with the people of God. We, too, wonder why we have to spend time there at all.

The desert serves as such a palpable analogy to the spiritual desert that we often find ourselves in and out of in this life.

Sometimes we bring the desert on ourselves by forgetting God. And sometimes we are surprised by the sudden appearance of desert all around us. We did not plan to go there. Things might have been going well for awhile ... then. Then the other shoe drops and there is nothing but death seemingly in front of us.

When my children and I were trying to navigate the new terrain of life we were thrust into, we did not know the way. The only map we had was God and His Word – oh, and many people offering counsel. Some good, some not so good.

Trying to acclimate to the spiritual desert we were in, it seemed like we just kept falling on cacti. One night, a little over a year of being in the desert, the LORD gave me a strong impression that I needed to pray for protection over my children and I. I stayed up until 4:00 in the morning praying and the next morning a friend called to ask what was going on in our world – she had begun praying at 4:00 in the morning the very same words I had been praying. A robbery had happened that night a couple doors down and my next door neighbor witnessed someone standing at the end of my driveway in the middle of the night.

I still shudder when I consider the mercy of God, calling me to pray fervently, and His protection over us. A couple weeks later, I witnessed eight men in two cars coming out of a neighbor's home. Another robbery. My heart melted within me. My son told me it was time I got a gun...

In the midst of an endless court battle, being falsely accused and sued by family members who felt they had a right to invade our lives while we suffered immensely, my health also took a turn for the worse. Autoimmune diseases all flared up, my strength was succumbing to the stress all around me. Finances were a wreck, our home was foreclosed upon, the robberies intensified our feelings of insecurity in an abyss of problems, so I went to buy a gun to protect my children and I.

Little did I know there was fine print on the back of a court document that said I could not purchase any firearms during the course of their investigation. Later this court error was fixed, but the trauma of this gun toting home-school mama being arrested, handcuffed and brought to jail was another thorn in the desert that I will not soon forget.

Oh God – do you see me? Do you see this turmoil we are in? How do You receive glory from this? Why is this happening? Joseph must have felt the same way – thrown in prison for a crime he did not commit. But He honored God in that desolate place **and he hoped**. When things go from bad to worse, we are never forgotten.
The thorns and thistles of life often grow on things of beauty.

It hurt more than I could ever convey to walk the lonely path we did, but in those broken cries and prayers to my God alone, there was this thing of beauty that He was accomplishing within. Endless hope in the character of God.

I thought I knew the LORD (and I did) before the biggest trial of my life, but now – now I knew Him in such an intimate way that all I wanted was His glory. I did not care how long He had me in this desert anymore. If this is where He wanted me, I surrendered my plans for an escape (it would not have worked, anyway), and worshiped Him right there in the dust. In the jail cell while the kind police officer explained the clerical error and vouched for my innocence. In the court while I was exposed to the most painful revelations a mother should never have to hear. In church when all I could do was weep and hide my face with my long hair to try and disguise my inner turmoil.

Just like God saw Ishmael's mom weeping for her son in the desert, God saw me. Raw and real, loved and embraced.

You see the secret of the desert is to not look at all the pain around us, but to look to the One Who made the desert. He has a purpose in the desert that far exceeds our purposes in the valley.

In the desert we discover that our perspective depends on what we look at – the problems or the promise around us.

God has life in the desert – not just death. We can be overflowing with hope even in the desert . . . because of the power of the Holy Spirit. The Holy Spirit also gave strength to Jesus when He was in the desert. And Jesus modeled surrender and worship in that place.

We are not alone in the desert, even though it feels so very lonely. Though it is tempting, don't look at the thorns around you – see the beauty in the desert and the oasis God provides for those who thirst after Him.

The pressure of our desert is making us into diamonds and the testimony formed is priceless.

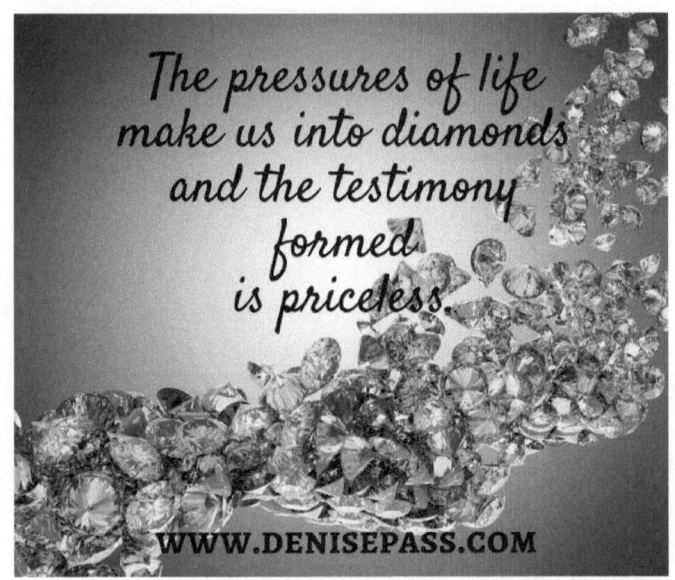

The next time you are in the desert, think of it as going camping with God. He is there with us. The Holy One – with us! The beauty of the desert is lost to those who just look at the rugged exterior. In the arid places, the places that seem like there is no more life at all, we have a new kind of hope forming within us – reinvented, made in the dry places – a thing of beauty to behold. A hope full of God's promises and fellowship – and our hopes and plans lie fallen on the desert floor. And we are free.

In the place of suffering and disbelief, even disillusionment, we can choose to not just survive, but thrive, even delight in God – Who meets us in the arid places of our lives. Pity parties are exposed, His purposes are seen as higher, and victory is found. This is where God longs for us to rest – not when things are perfect, but with Him in the desert – even when they are uncertain – to know that His blueprint for our lives is perfect at all times.

A Time to Worship

Oh Lord, we hope in You alone. Whether in the desert, the sunshine or the rain, You are our God in all of it.

We may as well sing while we are in the desert. Here is a worship song from Housefires – _Never Run Dry_

Day 5: Vision from the Pit - Purpose in Crisis

Inspirational Thought of the Day:
God can do miracles in the pits of life.

Scripture of the Day: Jeremiah 29:11-14
"For I know the plans I have for you, declares the LORD, plans for welfare and not for evil, to give you a future and a hope. Then you will call upon me and come and pray to me, and I will hear you. You will seek me and find me, when you seek me with all your heart. 14 I will make myself available to you,' says the Lord. 'Then I will reverse your plight and will regather you from all the nations and all the places where I have exiled you,' says the Lord. 'I will bring you back to the place from which I exiled you.'

We are still in the desert in here and things are heating up. In the place of dearth and scarcity, captivity and destruction – there is a promise.

Jeremiah stands as an example of trusting in God in devastating times. He understood God's sovereignty. He lived it out as the weeping prophet at times, but trusted his God because he knew His character and remembered the deeds of his God.

We are likely all familiar with this well known passage from the book of Jeremiah. Written to the exiles following their abduction from the home they loved and in that place of scorn, persecution and destruction, God sent a message to encourage them through His weeping prophet, Jeremiah. In a place of pain, God wanted them to flourish and enjoy life. Wow. It must have seemed crazy, God allowing them to suffer and promising a pending punishment, but telling them to prosper in that moment. Get comfortable in the pit?

Camped out in a land not their own, the Israelites must have wondered how they got to this place. They were God's chosen people – chosen for this? Have you ever felt that way? I sure have.

All too often we don't recognize how we have strayed from a path only to find we end up in a completely different place than our original destination. Or maybe someone else formed the path we are walking on that took us far away from our hopes and dreams. Can God's sovereignty reach this new place and make sense of our suffering? Definitely. But we might have to get comfortable in the pit.

It is hard to see beyond the pit. Feeling like we are enclosed with no way out, the path to victory is in surrender. If we seek to know our God, we know that He is faithful and nothing is wasted in His hands. His character is beyond our comprehension and every promise is always fulfilled. God is always good and His ways are good. But still we can doubt His purposes and think we might have a better plan. When we find ourselves struggling to get out of the pit, we might just be wrestling against God like Jacob did.

If God allowed the pit, He always has a purpose in it.

The question is whether or not we can trust Him in that place as well as in the place of blessing. The pit ultimately shaped the character of Joseph and elevated him to the second highest authority in Egypt. *God can do miracles in the pits of life.* He becomes our only source of strength as we are stripped from any other aid. In that isolation and temporary prison, He longs to be our Deliverer.

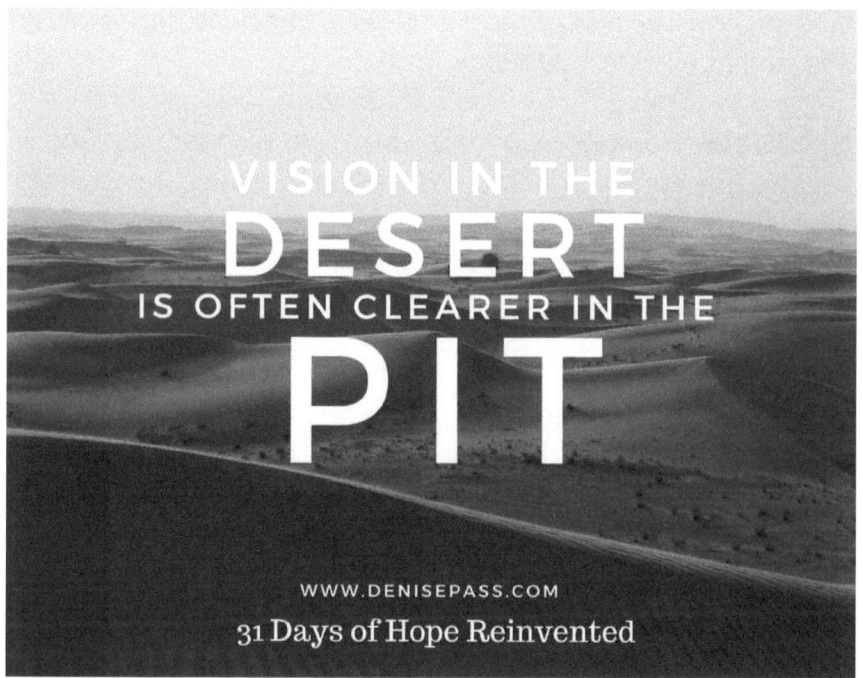

When we are sorry for the pit rather than seeking to understand His purpose in it, we might lengthen our stay there. Either way, God is with us in the pit and on the other side, as well. Accepting the pit, the desert, blessings – anything that comes from God's hand – We begin to understand His purposes are higher than our own.

It was in their suffering that God made Himself available to the Israelites. When they were blessed before, they had forgotten God and were distracted with things of lesser value. Hardship had gotten their attention and had revealed to them that they were missing what mattered most – knowing and enjoying God in this life that He gave – whether He blesses or He doesn't.

God wanted to bless His people again, but He cared more about their character and relationship with Himself than making their lives perfect. It actually would be cruel of God to do anything less.

Jeremiah had a pastor's heart and his people were suffering needlessly. Because they were also persecuting him and not surrendering to God's sovereign purpose, they were missing God's blessings.

God did not stop his crying, but He gave him hope during his grief and caught every single tear.

Like Jeremiah and God's people, you might wonder why God would say to enjoy life when life does not seem so enjoyable. You might apply these principles I have shared but still wish the pain did not visit you. That's ok. None of us delight in suffering and God understands. It is just learning to see beyond our circumstances and into what His sovereign purpose really means in our lives.

There is purpose in the tears. Jeremiah understands. Purpose in the pain. There as we gaze at our Savior, we see what He is accomplishing in our hearts. We become more like Him and suddenly our purpose is changed. We no longer want our way and start to understand that His ways are higher. We find His grace, His strength, our perfect peace – as we are wrapped in His perfect love.

When things seem to shift way off course, you can firmly know that God's plans never fail. You just might not like his plans at the moment, but when you recount what God has done in the past and what He has promised for the future, you can surrender to His purposes because of who He is.

God wants us to surrender to His sovereignty, rise above and understand what really matters, what the purpose of this life and our circumstances really are – about knowing and glorifying our good God.

While I thought I was living before "D-Day" in our home, now I see I was merely surviving. Somehow, instinctively I knew something was wrong. God was not going to leave his children in that place. He is too good for that.

Maybe your greatest sorrow is also your greatest deliverance.

Maybe another perspective just might help us to trust Him when we, too, have to drink the cup of suffering like Jesus did.

A Time to Worship

Lord, thank You for creating the pits in life to catch our attention and fix our gaze on You. When life hurts, ignite in our hearts Your purpose and help us to walk faithfully with you.

Here is a worship song for you to go with today's devotion: *In the Valley by Sovereign Grace Music.* When it seems the darkest, God's light shines to reveal His presence and purpose.

Inspirational Thought of the Day:
"In all the strife of life, no one can steal our hope except ourselves."

Scripture of the Day: Psalm 119:116
"Sustain me, my God, according to your promise, and I will live; do not let my hopes be dashed."

Hope is a necessary ingredient to life. Without it, we perish. The ultimate definition of hope, the daughter of faith, is trusting that God said He will do what He said He would. But sometimes we can feel that is for everyone else except ourselves.

Holding onto hope can take all we've got sometimes. So many things in this fallen world threaten hope's survival. Maybe we are in the desert, seemingly with no end in sight and just find it too difficult to dare to hope. Maybe we are on the other side of a significant trial but are afraid to hope. Circumstances, discouragement and fear can surely hold us back from hope, but they are birthed in an environment all our own.

It might help to know where we stand, to set expectations aright. We are **hated** by an enemy who delights to steal our joy and hope, because he is angry that He can never take away our salvation.

He will settle for wrecking our witness or get us sidetracked with trivial matters, but he really wants to discourage us from having hope at all. If he achieves this goal, God's people go through life living defeated lives, without hope and ineffective to share God's hope with others because our own hope has been extinguished.

Added to our enemy's activity of destroying hope in us is his influence on others who are used, sometimes unknowingly – to try and dash our hopes, too. Who would want to do that, right? But we do it all the time when we try to discourage a brother or sister in the work of the LORD in their lives.

Naivety gone, we recognize we are surrounded by enemies, but we might not readily see the enemy within. Sounds dramatic, I know. But what we do with the pressures in this life that try to snuff out hope is on us. It is not easy to stand up to all of the attacks on maintaining our hope in God, but it is a fight God can help us to wage and win. So, who's the Thief? Who is it that ultimately steals our hope?

Satan, Satan working through people, circumstances – they contribute to our downfall, but there is another thief we do not recognize, because wait for it – it is ourselves. Why would we bear the blame – why would we ever want to harm ourselves or take away our hope?

Sure, the instigator was likely from another source, but what we do with the "hope killer" is our choice alone. We must consider where our hope is placed. Is it in others, ourselves or in the only One who is capable of making and keeping promises?

Here are some "Hope Builders" that have greatly helped me to hold onto hope:

Where our hope is placed. When hope is in Christ alone, we have a consistent source that does not sway with man's fickle opinion or momentary circumstances. *Reinvented hope is not dependent on a temporary goal or the success of achieving that goal – it is fixed on the author of hope itself.*

Recognizing the battle and its source. People's opinions are often formed in jealousy. Jealousy is hatred. Discouragement, gossip and negativity only come from one place – they are of the devil. His end is certain. Dismiss attacks from people or the devil as being evil and having a just end. *God already waged war against the enemy of our souls – satan is defeated and our hope is secure.*

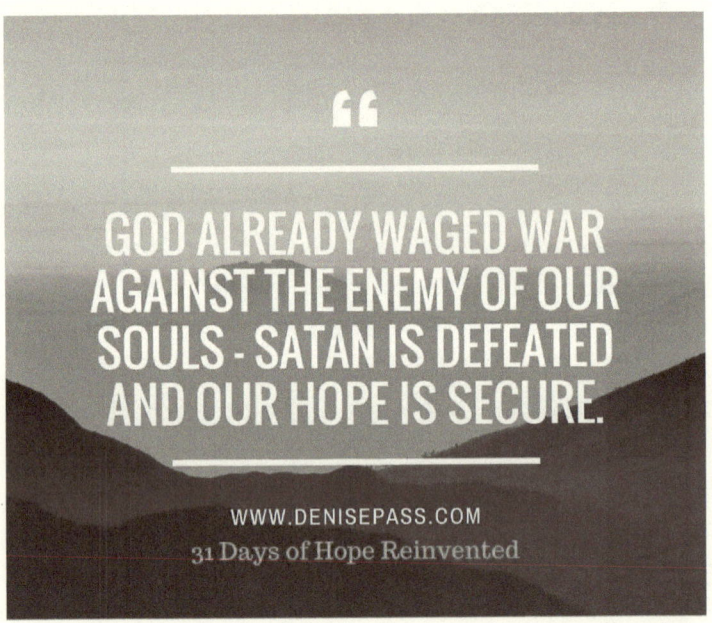

Pressing in and seeking God's promises. Reality hits us square in the eye and sometimes it can be LOUD. We don't have to **let** life's troubles confuse us, even though they are convincing that hope seems like a futile effort. We have to go against our feelings and place our hope firmly in the hands of God's word. *It is hard work keeping the flames of hope alive, but God's promises fuel that hope.*

Crying out to God. We need help in this quest for this hope from another world. It is found only in relationship with Christ. *Crying out for help and perspective helps us to overcome and triumph over hopelessness or false hope that always disappoints.*

Instead of adopting the world's hope, we begin to see formed this new **Reinvented Hope** as we gain God's view instead of our own.

Focusing on God and His Word, not the hope killers around us. This one is a tough one when our hope killers are not just in our mind, but flesh around us, focused on tearing us down. When we listen to the voices all around us instead of to the voice of the Holy Spirit, we easily succumb to the strategy of the enemy.

In all the strife of life, no one can steal our hope except ourselves. We have to get up and fight and resist pouring over the negativity of other people or our own self-doubt and insecurity. A great assurance for this soul is that *nothing in this world can take away our hope – it is impossible, for our hope is certain.* We might feel like hope is gone, but it never is for those whose hope is in God. *Picking up the pieces of our shattered hope, we form it into a new hope that never disappoints.*

A Time to Worship

Cornerstone by Hillsong is a worship song that reminds us where our hope needs to be placed. Worship Him, our God of Reinvented Hope, a hope given to us through the resurrection of Jesus Christ from the dead. Hope is alive!

Lord, thank You for keeping our hope secure in You. Help us to hold on to Your promises firmly.

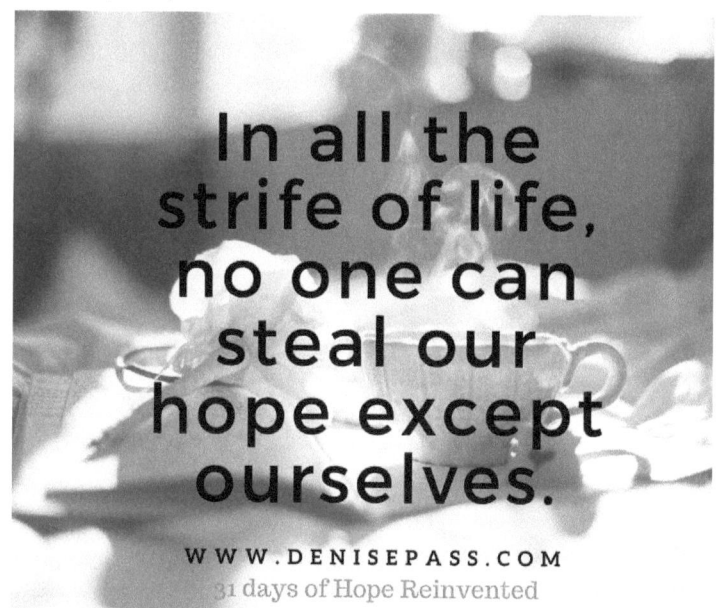

Inspirational Thought of the Day:
At the heart of our recovery is a belief in the God who reshapes our hopes and expectations into His own.

Scriptures of the Day:
Psalm 41:11
"Why, my soul, are you downcast? Why so disturbed within me? Put your hope in God, for I will yet praise him, my Savior and my God.

Psalms 40:1-3
"I waited patiently for the LORD; he inclined to me and heard my cry. He drew me up from the pit of destruction, out of the miry bog, and set my feet upon a rock, making my steps secure. He put a new song in my mouth, a song of praise to our God. Many will see and fear, and put their trust in the LORD."

Today's topic I tread on carefully. The "loneliness of soul" as depression has been called, is so characterized because it is often so misunderstood.

Shame and self hatred can often come with depression, as this emotional pain is just as significant as physical pain, but we can feel judged and isolated to admit such a profession.

Ever been really discouraged to the point where you just did not have any hope at all? Maybe feel as if you are gasping for air and trying to find hope and meaning, only to be confronted with a wave of strong emotions that threaten to engulf you? Add to these feelings the stigma of depression and it seems there is no way out.

The battle in the mind to overcome negative or sad emotions is real. The motivation to escape the prison of depression can falter as people are overwhelmed with sadness or grief and feel powerless to affect it at all.

Depression is real. Causes can stem from circumstances, sin, a chemical imbalance, mental disorder or our own spiritual battle, to name a few. Fixing depression is not as easy as a band-aid on a physical infirmity that we readily can affect, but God can do all things.

The One Who fearfully and wonderfully made us also chose to be encased in human flesh and can identify with every sorrow and heartbreak we have.

Some of God's greatest servants encountered depression – but they did not all stay there. David is such an encouragement to me. He confessed and was honest about being depressed, anxious and stressed. Who wouldn't be in his situation? David knew what it was to suffer greatly, chased in the desert for fifteen years by a mad man who was also depressed.

Sometimes even other depressed people can try to bring us down with them, preoccupied with self and ascribing motives to us that just don't exist. Saul was crazed with jealousy of David and left those thoughts unchecked, fueling them with his false perceptions. Our minds can really get in a fog if we take in the lies and negativity and allow it to go unchecked.

But David's refuge was God's word. He did not have a local CVS to run to or Dr. Phil to cheer him up. Hiding in caves, despairing of life – His medicine was to run to God and His word and to cry out to Him.

While sometimes medicine is needed and a great help to sufferers of depression, the greatest healing balm I have found is being in God's presence reading His word and crying out to Him, just like David modeled for us all.

My visit down depression lane has been brief and intermittent. Personal choices I made while there were what determined how long I stayed and when I would be leaving.

Recognition. A lot of times we don't see that we have a choice. We don't realize the state of mind we are in. Walking around in a cloud and sad atmosphere, we are often unaware of and don't recognize that we are depressed. The first step toward leaving the path of depression was to recognize we are on that path in the first place. With 50,000 to 70,000 thoughts going through our mind in one day, sometimes seeing the source of those thoughts can be dizzying.

Roots. Finding the root of depression helps us to see. If we take those thoughts and examine where they came from, we begin to see the culprit that served as a catalyst in the formation of depression. Painful roots can be lifted out of the dust, healed and transplanted again in the healthier soil of being rooted in God's love, instead.

Relationship. Victory out of depression is a daily battle in the mind that we often cannot fight by ourselves. We have to fight and choose to overcome, but if we are in a bad state of mind, we might need others to pluck us out and help us gain perspective.

Rescue. Seeing motivations of ourselves and others through biblical and prayer filters helps us to release possession of our thoughts and surrender them to Jesus. Placing them in God's hands – sometimes again and again – is when we begin to see things from His perspective.

Real Hope. We need to tell ourselves the truth. The many discouraging thoughts are not always true. They might be convincing, but lies, nonetheless.

This is not going to last forever. As long as we want change and are willing to be on the hunt for healing, your hope is sure and changed. The hope we have in Christ is abiding and eternal. Where we are now is not.

Trying to escape depression with a fake hope just won't work. Happy little phrases and anecdotes are not a real solution. But we are never without hope if we approach our internal struggles biblically. What does His word say? Reflecting on His promises rather than our ever-looming reality is a life preserver ready to be used, if we let it be.

The circumstances surrounding the revelation of my children being harmed provoked depression and overwhelming grief that seemed insurmountable. My expectations were blown out of the water and I could not see how I could ever recover. If it had not been for God's presence before and throughout, surely I would not have survived.

The night before the revelation of sin in our family, God awoke me to write a song. Usually my heart is filled with praise when I write Him a song, but this night my soul was in anguish. Complete fear gripped my heart and the LORD began to reveal to me that my life was going to change dramatically. I did not know that as I wrote the song and sought God's face, the father of my children was harming one of my children in that moment.

The next day the LORD walked with me as truth was unfolding that broke our hearts and rocked our world. Shock and horror filled my heart and I felt I was not even in my body. The stress added to the pain and brought all of my autoimmune diseases out of remission.

Trying to function with simple tasks felt impossible. It was in this place of despair that my brain would not turn off. Sleeping was difficult, anxiety consumed me over the constant barrage of attacks, accusations and court dates.

The ominous doorbell ringing again and again with more subpoenas frightened my children and I as we felt like puppets on strings being thrown around carelessly through a process we did not ask for.

Deep sadness emanates often from a place of suffering. It threatens to snuff out hope with the grim reality of its tentacles wrapping around our mind again and again, proliferating a message of doubt and hopelessness.

But we need not be trapped by depression's lure. The choice depends on us, if we will see the escape. *God's love reaches deeper than the deepest pit and demolishes the lies that depression tells us.*

At the core of depression can be unbelief formed in the chasm of broken expectations. At the heart of our recovery is a belief in the God who reshapes our hopes and expectations into His own.

We become disheartened when life has not lived up to what we hoped for. We are set free when we realize it is not our life, after all. Sadness for self is removed when we don the attitude and reality that our lives are wrapped up in Christ's. If we really believe that we no longer live but that Christ lives through us, then we see our lives as living for One.

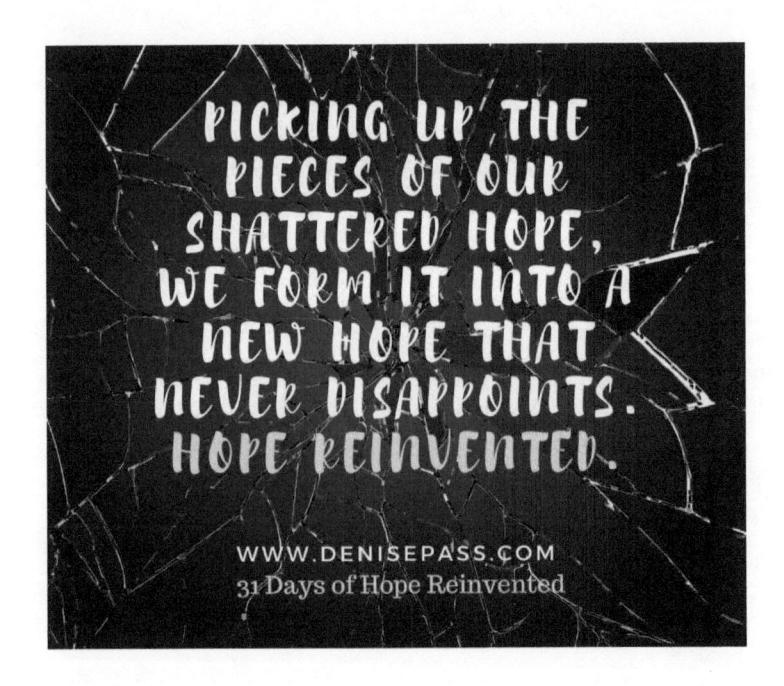

> PICKING UP THE PIECES OF OUR SHATTERED HOPE, WE FORM IT INTO A NEW HOPE THAT NEVER DISAPPOINTS. HOPE REINVENTED.
>
> WWW.DENISEPASS.COM
> 31 Days of Hope Reinvented

Adopting the mind of Christ is paramount to overcoming thoughts in a mind filled with troubling thoughts. Christ sought to glorify the Father. He did not consider Himself, but only others around Him. His zeal for God consumed Him.

If we are real, zeal for self can often consume us. God knows that. He wants us to lift up our eyes to Him and see where our help comes from. Self can be a burden, but we are free when we can lay self down and see our problems as potential to glorify God in it.

Moving past depression is not easy, but it is possible. Feelings are powerful, but they are not more powerful than God's Word, which never returns void.

Rather than desiring an escape from pain, we can ask for God to be with us in the pain and to give us His perspective as we navigate through the mire of emotions and pain. The more we seek God, the more we get answers to our questions. The more we ask, the more we receive. God is not limited by our limits and the Maker of us all has the remedy for every suffering – emotional or physical.

A Time to Worship

The song, <u>*Draw Me Near*</u> was the song I wrote on the night before my life and the life of my children was changed forever and now serves as a reminder of God's faithfulness at all times. If our hope is in anything other than God, our emotions ride a roller-coaster.

Lord, help us to trust You with our emotions. You made our hearts and can heal them, too.

Day 8: Facing Disillusionment

31 Days of Hope Reinvented

Inspirational Thought of the Day:
Confusion comes in when our definition of good does not fit God's.

Scriptures of the Day:
Proverbs 13:22
"Hope deferred makes the heart sick, but a longing fulfilled is a tree of life."

1 Peter 4:12 (NIV)
"Dear friends, do not be surprised at the fiery ordeal that has come on you to test you, as though something strange were happening to you. 13 But rejoice inasmuch as you participate in the sufferings of Christ, so that you may be overjoyed when his glory is revealed."

Psalm 73 (all)

Like the desert, there is beauty in the forest, but if we focus on each individual tree, we might miss the big picture. Sometimes, we can't see the forest for the trees. We started on this path simply enough, but somehow in the maze of life we ended up lost in the woods, not sure we will ever find our way out.

Disillusionment is tied not just to failed expectations we have for life, but to our inability to control those outcomes.

Disillusionment chokes out hope as we suffocate on what could or should have been. When we are unable to process or accept our circumstances and wonder where God is in it all, hope still remains – cloaked in a different garb.

If we walk with God, we have His strength to cling to in challenging seasons of life, but disillusionment can damage that faith and create space for idolatry if we are not careful – as we try to cling to what we wanted instead. *Trying to hold onto our dreams as if we are owed them is ultimately a lack of trust in God.*

Trusting the LORD when times are good comes easily, but it is in the rocky ravines that we need to understand His purposes are far wider and greater than a temporary stay in a craggy landscape.

When we want to hope, to believe that God is still good but we are surrounded by death and uncertainty, how do we survive the land of disillusionment without getting a jaded heart?   *By discovering a new hope.*

When faced with his grim reality and the flourishing of the wicked, David said his "feet had almost slipped". He described his affliction as "All day long I have been afflicted, and every morning brings new punishments". This kind of hardship was way beyond hope deferred and not getting his own way. Way out of the league of the troubles that Peter spoke of, too, which are common to man. This was deep suffering. David refrained from speaking the raw truth of his anguish and doubt out loud – he struggled to believe he could even have the thoughts he was having – but he did.

It troubled him deeply that the wicked thrived while he sought to obey God. It did not seem fair. God's character and His will were on the table to be evaluated … UNTIL. Until he came into God's sanctuary – into His presence – and understood <u>the</u> end and their end.

It was there that He saw God's goodness even while life hurt. He felt God's presence and knew instinctively that God was with him in the fiery trials and that He held him in His right hand. As we begin to face all the potential sinful outcomes that traumatic events can bring into our lives, we begin the process of healing. Are we bitter or angry with God? Let's be honest – our faith is hurt and we often attempt to hide our hurt from God when He allows suffering to collide with our paths. Understanding the role that God's sovereignty plays in our disillusionment helps us to face it instead of avoiding it or becoming numb to our pain.

God's sovereignty is not something we can fully comprehend. How is it that He knows everything before it happens – and yet still allows something in that we disapprove of? Looking at the foundation of the plans for our life can help us to better understand our path. At the inception of our hopes and dreams, where was God? Was He inspiring our hearts to do His will, or were we inviting him to our dream and asking for His favor and blessing?

An encounter with God puts everything into perspective. While I mourned my broken life and the testimony I never wanted, God revealed His hope for me. He created us for His glory, yet somehow while I wept for my children and myself, I forgot it was all about His glory, not mine. Like David, I looked at other people prospering and wondered why I was so messed up. I did not plan my life this way. Oh. Yeah. I guess that statement is revealing, too, huh?

I longed to be like the other happy couples who never had to walk the dark cold court hall toward a divorce that was never supposed to happen. How did I get into this forest full of problems? Could God raise me from these ashes? Yes, but even better, He could reveal to me that even the hope of deliverance was not the hope that He wanted me to have.

I had to let go of the grief in one hand to grab hold of God's hope for the future, but I was afraid. If God would allow this kind of intense suffering, could He be trusted? Yes, but I had to die first. My hope had to die in order to get a new reinvented hope in Jesus.

Dying to my hopes was a long, arduous death. Lots of chocolate (yes, I am bringing up the "c" word again), tears and disbelief.

But holding onto that old hope was killing me inside and no amount of therapy, chocolate (notice a pattern here?) or buffalo wings could heal me. Only God could, but I Had. To. Let. Go. *Completely.*

Not my will, LORD. Not my will. All my hopes and dreams I lay at Your feet. You made me and You know what's best. Help my unbelief and cause my heart to want Your hope and not my own.
God's plans don't make sense to us because our plans often come from a place of being self-oriented and formed in a desire for our comfort.

Confusion comes in when our definition of good does not fit God's. But when we come into His presence seeking to understand, he shows us that His thoughts and ways are much higher. And maybe, just maybe, it is actually His mercy.

When I was disillusioned and doubted whether I could trust Christ for the suffering He permitted in my life, He reminded me that He suffered, too. He understood. I had lost sight of what really matters – His glory. Not my reputation or the social stigma. Not that my pain did not matter to God, but somehow in the mess I was in, God needed to receive glory. It was not about me, after all.

A Time to Worship

This song, *Thy Will Be Done by Hillary Scott* is a song that really ministers at the place of disillusionment.

Lord, You never leave us without hope. Thank You for giving us a new hope in You.

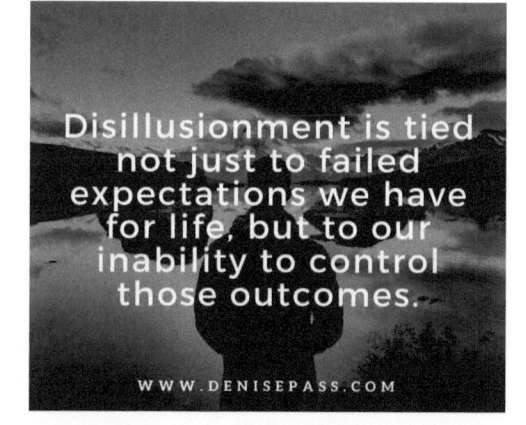

> Disillusionment is tied not just to failed expectations we have for life, but to our inability to control those outcomes.
>
> WWW.DENISEPASS.COM

DAY 9: FACING FEAR

31 Days of Hope Reinvented

WWW.DENISEPASS.COM

Inspirational Thought of the Day:
We face fear when we see its potential consequences, place them in God's hands and adopt His hope, instead.

Scripture of the Day:

Proverbs 23:18
"Surely there is a future, and your hope will not be cut off."

Psalm 119:116
"Sustain me according to your promise, and I will live; do not let my hopes be dashed."

The only thing we have to fear is fear itself.

Franklin D. Roosevelt's words from his first inaugural address still profoundly convey a truth that exposes fear's impact. Fear has been a foe of mine for some time. Over and over again it would rise up, taunting me with its threats. It promised destruction and failure. It spoke of an end to hope and propagated a message of being forgotten or forsaken. It left a lingering feeling of uncertainty and insecurity.

Fear grips our hearts and minds and threatens to paralyze us from moving forward in life. When we give in to fear, we let it rule us and limit the life God has for us.

Fear is formed in the midst of a disruption of our hope for our life. Struggling to put together the pieces of our broken dreams, we grasp onto a counterfeit hope and try to build again. We fake a smile or try to pretend the fear building inside of us does not exist. We try to placate the fear with a substitute hope, but it just does not work. God has something better to help us overcome fear and restore a new hope.

Instead of trying to escape fear, we can look at it square in the eyes and speak to it in light of what God says about our hope and future. *Fear is intimidating, but in the face of perfect love, it is cast out.*

When fear attempts to consume us, God's word speaks a living promise.

Isaiah 34:4
"Say to those with fearful hearts, 'Be strong, do not fear; your God will come, he will come with vengeance; with divine retribution he will come to save you.'"

The gavel fell and my heart pounded within me. My children would have to testify in court. The asthma which was formerly in remission tightened its noose around me and I struggled to breathe. Looking around the room, I felt the piercing stare of hatred from those who pursued me relentlessly.

Trying to maintain control over my emotions, I silently prayed for God to give me strength to not give in to fear. He overwhelmed me with His grace and strength. I did not want to endure the suffering I had feared, but I learned to trust Him when the path hurts that He has me on and to approach fear with God's grace instead of my own strength.

My heart hurt so desperately for my children and I wanted to spare them, but in that moment the LORD told me that they were His and He would enable them.

Sometimes we don't want to have to walk through the door of fear, but until we walk through it we cannot see the victory and hope that God has for us on the other side.

Ultimately, God granted victory, but more important than the victory in court was the victory over broken hope and the creation of a firm hope in Him.

Fear can take on a life of its own. Fear feels so very real and sometimes it is not based on reality at all. Either way, there is a way out and it is not through our own manufactured hope.

We face fear when we see its potential consequences, place them in God's hands and adopt His hope, instead.

A Time to Worship

The song, <u>Whom Shall I Fear by Chris Tomlin</u> encourages us to trust God, the One Who commands armies and Who is in control.

Rather than fearing losing what we planned or hoped for, we have an alternative that never fails. If we give our hopes and fears to God, He can show us another kind of hope that is based on His goodness and mercy, rather than our gain.

Lord, thank You for revealing Your goodness and hope to us. Help us to trust you when we are filled with fear and fill us with Your hope and joy instead.

> We face fear when we see its potential consequences, place it in God's hands and adopt His hope, instead.
>
> WWW.DENISEPASS.COM

Day 10: Facing Judgement

31 Days of Hope Reinvented

Inspirational Thought of the Day:
Hope was never meant to come from man, for we were made for another world where hope never fades or disappoints.

Scripture of the Day: Psalm 25:3
"No one whose hope is in you will ever be put to shame."

Distractions from our healing come from familiar places. Wanting to be accepted and feeling ashamed of our troubles only causes further devastation when wagging tongues share our hurt far and wide. Slander and libel only make matters worse. Multiply the devastation many times over for someone who naturally is a people pleaser. What is God's purpose in this? God's people know what it is like to be mischaracterized or misjudged.

Proverbs 19:22 says what a person desires is unfailing love, but so often a critical spirit is more plentiful. Just to be accepted for who we are – in all our quirks and individuality – is a deep desire God placed within us.

The longing to be "ok" is aggravated by an inconsistent world where normal doesn't truly exist.

While man still feels the need to compare and judge, God is calling out to our souls with a message of unconditional love and acceptance.

Whether we have suffered a traumatic event or not, our hope takes some bruises along the road of life. Probably one of the most painful aspects of recovering our hope is the people around us who keep us in a place of hopelessness by their judgment. We cannot stand up to judgment when it is not based in reality. The only way to overcome self-judgment and the judgment of others is to lay it down.

How? The Bible says an undeserved curse falls right off our shoulder and that we ought not to let another man judge us (Colossians 2:16). The choice is ours. Sometimes we continue to pick it back up, punishing ourselves. If we are not careful, this judgment forms a deep shame within us that brings deep discouragement that seems irreparable.

When my children and I were thrust into our new reality, the one place where we should have felt safe – church – became a painful place. We felt less than, isolated and categorized in a group of "those" people. Sometimes people mean well, but don't see that they are actually worsening the situation.

When people tread in the place of thinking they know another person's heart they stand dangerously in a position of self-righteous pride. They cannot walk in another person's shoes and certainly cannot be their Holy Spirit.

In those times when we feel misunderstood, our hope for acceptance can be laid on the altar and we can pick up Christ's view of us, instead. Laying down the idol of the opinion of man, we start to see our hope was in the wrong place to begin with.

Reinvented hope does not rely on man's affirmation – it's foundation is in a completely different place and it's goal has shifted to being all for God's glory.

Haughty stares and people gossiping behind our back can still bum us out, but now we know where our real hope comes from. Hope was never meant to come from man, for we were made for another world where hope never fades or disappoints.

A Time to Worship

The song, *No Longer Slaves by Bethel Worship* is such an encouragement . . . to know that we are a part of God's family forever. Accepted unconditionally. Freedom indeed!

Lord, thank You for covering our shame and exposing us to Your abiding hope, instead.

> WHEN WE FEEL Misunderstood, OUR HOPE FOR Acceptance CAN BE LAID AT THE ALTAR WHERE WE PICK UP GOD'S VIEW OF US, INSTEAD.
> WWW.DENISEPASS.COM

Day 11: Facing the Sin Within

Inspirational Thought of the Day:
It was not just other people's actions that hurt us – it was our hope that also suffered a crushing blow.

Scripture of the Day: Psalm 130:7
"O Israel, hope in the Lord! For with the Lord there is steadfast love, and with him is plentiful redemption."

Sometimes we can get so caught up in the pain others have inflicted on us that we don't take the time to gaze in the mirror. Sure, it is not always a 50/50 blame game, but is there a fraction that we might be culpable for that we need to examine?

Being a victim is not the path to victory. Even though grief may last for a season and healing is needed and real, part of that healing is seeing where we may have stumbled as a result of someone else's sin against us. Exposing our own sin helps us to have compassion on those who hurt us and to begin to unpack sin's impact on us, as well.

Looking at the sin within ourselves does not minimize the responsibility of others, but frees us from the grip that sin might have on us.

The burden of sin keeps us from genuine hope when we are consumed with another person's actions and the hurt they brought into our lives.

At the onset of the examination of ourselves, we see the surface. We can try to cover it up with makeup or look to see the source below. Why do the actions of others hurt us so deeply? Layer upon layer we try to cover our hurt to keep the raw truth from being exposed. *It was not just other people's actions that hurt us – it was our hope that also suffered a crushing blow.* Recovering from that reality can prove to be too much to bear. A people without hope perish.

In our attempts to try and rejuvenate our hope, we allow other things to creep in – bitterness, disillusionment, fear and ... hopelessness. Unless we are willing to gaze into God's word for illumination into our soul to really understand our condition of despair, we will go from one false hope to another.

Recovery from a traumatic event is long and deep. Prolonged recovery from any hurt can really cause our hope to waiver. But there is good news in this place of admitting our hopes are all but gone. At the end of ourselves, we no longer have to work to try and manufacture our own hope. Instead, God gives us His hope – eternal and perfect.

A Time to Worship

Let's worship the LORD Who is there with us in the deep waters and makes a way for us. The song, *Oceans* is such a vivid reminder of letting go and trusting God in the deep places of our lives where we are overwhelmed.

Lord, thank You for healing us from the inside out. Thank You for taking our fragile hope and reforming it into a hope in You alone.

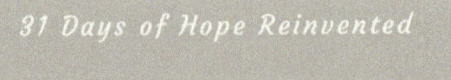

Day 12: Facing Memories Through a Biblical Lens

31 Days of Hope Reinvented

Inspirational Thought of the Day:
God still wants to take that place of pain and redeem it into a living testimony rather than a dead memory that comes back to haunt us with sorrow.

Scripture of the Day: Isaiah 40:31
"But those who hope in the Lord will renew their strength. They will soar on wings like eagles; they will run and not grow weary, they will walk and not be faint."

In the wake of all of life's experiences, there are reminders that pop up from time to time. Memories jarred from a song that is heard, a familiar smell, a place, a name…sometimes at the most inopportune times.

When we try to move forward in our lives and the past keeps resurfacing, our newly formed hope can feel fragile.

Past memories threaten to steal the lessons we have learned and imprison us back into the state we were in that we never wanted to encounter again. But God.

Sometimes it feels like the LORD purposely has us face again and again things we would rather forget. It can feel cruel and tortuous. But God *loves us too much to allow us to stay trapped in a place where we only feel safe if we block out any hint of our former pain.*

When we are reminded of past mistakes or burdens, He whispers hope and a different perspective. The accusations from yesterday are changed in His presence and understood to be His grace, instead.

Failures are seen as vehicles that brought us to see our need of God rather than to separate us from Him.

At times it is necessary to remove ourselves from abusive relationships or situations that really aren't healthy for us.

God still wants to take that place of pain and redeem it into a living testimony rather than a dead memory that comes back to haunt us with sorrow.

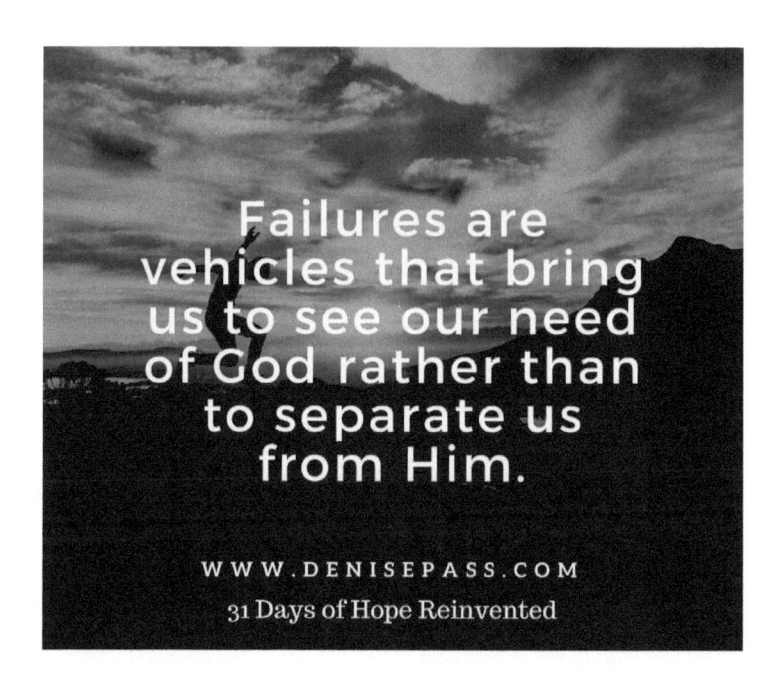

> **Failures are vehicles that bring us to see our need of God rather than to separate us from Him.**
>
> WWW.DENISEPASS.COM
> 31 Days of Hope Reinvented

> GOD WANTS TO TAKE THAT PLACE OF PAIN AND REDEEM IT INTO A LIVING TESTIMONY RATHER THAN A DEAD MEMORY THAT COMES BACK TO HAUNT US WITH SORROW.
>
> www.denisepass.com
> 31 Days of Hope Reinvented

When we are overcome with our past, finding Scriptures to infuse with what we falsely believed opens our eyes and helps us to process memories in light of God's never-ending hope.

Viewing the past through His lens – His Word – helps us to make sense of life's messes.

The past may never be something we understand, but we can come to a place of peace as we see God's purposes in it. And His purposes are always good, always higher than we could ever imagine.

God is a Redeemer of all things. Former things have passed away, but in the corner of our minds He wants to take that piece of our hope that was ripped apart and restore it.

Until we let go of the past, we cannot grab a hold of the new hope that the present offers.

The past cannot keep us, the present is evaporating, but our future hope is certain.

Looking ahead, we are informed by the past enough to see that the God who brought us through it can also guide us through whatever life brings.

As we look over the landscape of life, we will see how He weaves it all together into a beautiful masterpiece – both the rugged and the beautiful pieces forming a vessel perfected for the LORD's glory.

A Time to Worship

This song by Casting Crowns really says it well. <u>Already There.</u> Trust God with your past and the future. None of it is wasted.

Lord, thank You for making a highway in the wilderness, a place of rest for us when we are weary and lost. No matter what the past says, You already know the end.

> THE PAST MAY NEVER BE SOMETHING WE UNDERSTAND, BUT WE CAN COME TO A PLACE OF PEACE AS WE SEE GOD'S PURPOSES IN IT.
>
> www.denisepass.com
> 31 Days of Hope Reinvented

31 Days of Hope Reinvented

Day 13: Facing the Enemy

Inspirational Thought of the Day:
Ultimately victory cannot be won if we do not even know what we are aiming at.

Scripture of the Day:
Psalm 119:114
"You are my refuge and my shield; I have put my hope in your word."

The enemy lines are drawn and we think we know the enemy's tactics. Adrenaline pumping through our veins, we brace ourselves for the next attack and prepare our own offensive strategy . . .

. . . Or maybe we are wandering out on the field unaware that we are standing in the middle of a battleground. Yep. That is more like me.

Pelted with attack after attack we cannot fathom that anyone could be so manipulative or conniving. But we better wise up, because there is no sign of things letting up and we don't want to be another casualty on the field of life, strewn with people who lost their hope and let the enemy take it from them. What we need is a strategy. *Though we feel weakened, God is calling us to rise up and fight.*

How do we fight? What does this fighting look like? David has some ideas to share with us. He prayed and asked God to deal with his enemies. Though he entered into God's presence stressed and wanting vengeance, he left God's presence keenly aware of the mercy that had been extended to Him.

Wise up. Ever had someone believe the worst in you or relentlessly attack you? You kind of wonder if there is a sign on your back, saying, "kick me while I am down", right? The fool keeps on going and suffers for it, though, and we need to be spiritually discerning to understand our enemies tactics, how to counter them, as well as who, in fact, is our enemy. The moment of revelation is sobering when we realize we have another enemy in the ranks – especially when they claim to be our friend. Jesus understands. One He loved and washed the feet of betrayed him with a kiss.

Get over it. Hurt can paralyze us if we let it. *We have to get over the reality of the betrayal to be able to see clearly.* God knows it hurts but that *hurt can be a tool to help us or a vessel to trap us with bitterness and pain.*

We have to get over the reality of the betrayal to be able to see clearly.

www.denisepass.com
31 Days to Hope Reinvented

Motivations. Trying to get into the heart and mind of one who has us under siege proves difficult, but God's word opens our eyes to a spiritual understanding that trumps the world's perspective every time. The motivations of another person just don't matter. Let God deal with that. What matters is our response to their affront or attack.

Stick to the facts. People might intend harm and they might not. *We can get lost walking in a mine field if we try to guess the motivations of another.* Only God knows that. Sticking to the facts keeps us from the dangerous territory of presumption, which is a real joy and hope killer. It is a lot easier to understand objective facts rather than subjective ideas.

No blaming. Blaming comes naturally to us. It is easier to think that we do not bear the responsibility, and somehow makes us feel better to cast aspersions on the other wicked people. Sometimes we truly don't bear responsibility for an attack. But blaming cannot erase the pain or fix our heartache. Instead of blaming, we can pour out our heart to God and ask for His understanding.

No hiding. *Trying to destroy the evidence of our broken heart will not rid us of the scar it has left behind – it will only cause our hearts to harden.* Pretending just does not work for long. Exposing our responses to our enemies helps us to be real. *Ultimately victory cannot be won if we do not even know what we are aiming at.*

No Benedict Arnold. Don't play into the enemy's tactics. The enemy of our soul is cunning and comes like an angel of light. He trips us up to sin then condemns us and blames us. He uses other people, too. We don't have to let them provoke us or cause us to stumble – that is defeating ourselves.

Be strong. I love the verses in Joshua reminding him over and over again to be strong and courageous. The strength is available to us, but we have to come to God and His Word to get it.

Let Him Fight For You. Today's scripture is not just a nice poetic illustration. It is real. He is our refuge. He is our shield – if our hope truly is in His Word. What does that mean?

It means I confess doubt and place everything in His hands. I hunt for verses that speak life and truth and surrender my way to His. We have the God of the universe fighting for us and can take authority over the enemy in Jesus' name.

So, who is our enemy? It might be an illness, another person, ourselves, or even a fellow believer who poses as an enemy in our lives. But the real enemy is the devil, seeking to use anything at his disposal to destroy us.

Sometimes we are our own worst enemy and sometimes we let people beat us up. That's not what God wants for us. We can rise above attacks and glorify God in them by overcoming evil with good. Fighting for our enemies in prayer and asking God to reveal their sins as well as our own sends the devil packing. Let's fight on our knees together and see what God does. Our victory is sure.

A Time to Worship

This song is a great reminder that our God is for us and more than that, He is fighting for us: *God is Fighting For Us by Hillsong*

Lord, thank You for overcoming every enemy we will ever face. Help us to let go of a vain hope in vengeance and to have our hope in You and Your word alone.

Day 14: Facing and Embracing Reality – The New Normal

31 Days of Hope Reinvented

Inspirational Thought of the Day:
Change is a stepping stone in the path of life that is necessary for our final destination.

Scripture of the Day:
Psalm 37:9
"Those who hope in the LORD will inherit the land."

Coming to grips with our new normal is no easy task. We are creatures of habit and prefer comfort and stability to change – especially if that change is abrupt and unwelcome.

But while we are waiting for our circumstances to change, looking to the future is not our only solace. Right smack dab in the middle of our new normal we can be more than content, but also at peace – knowing we are exactly where God has us to be in that moment.

This truth might also create some misunderstanding between ourselves and God. Why would He allow it? Can't He see that we are uncomfortable?

In a land not their own, the Israelites wondered if they would ever reach the promised land. Many of them didn't. They did not like God's provision, doubted His goodness and His promises. It did not make sense that they should stay so long hanging out in a seemingly purposeless trip in the desert, yet they determined the length of their stay by their actions.

If our chief goal is to glorify God with our lives, then we *don't just accept our new normal, but embrace it as being in God's will for a purpose much higher than our own.*

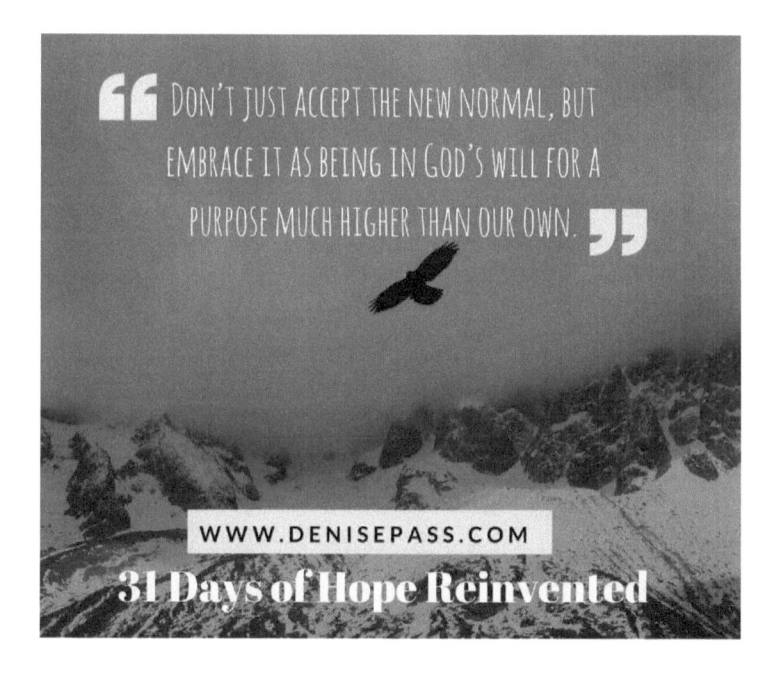

> "DON'T JUST ACCEPT THE NEW NORMAL, BUT EMBRACE IT AS BEING IN GOD'S WILL FOR A PURPOSE MUCH HIGHER THAN OUR OWN."
>
> WWW.DENISEPASS.COM
> 31 Days of Hope Reinvented

Hanging onto yesterday will leave us discontented and ineffective for the Kingdom of God. But being Kingdom-minded will help us to have a perspective that thrives when things around us are unsettling and uncertain.

Did we somehow forget that our stay here is a temporary one? This is not our home. Having a mentality of flexibility helps us to *process change and view it as a stepping stone in the path of life that is necessary for our final destination.*

Each presumed off-course path that we take is instead a fulfillment of our calling. Will we accept our mission?

> Past memories threaten to steal the lessons we learned & imprison us back into the state we were in.
>
> Walk on.

Having our hope in the character of God enables us to overcome a lack of faith when it seems we have been forgotten.

We hold firmly to God's hope because of His character behind His promises. He cannot be unfaithful - it is impossible for Him to do so.

If we could see the end goal of where God is bringing us to, we would not try to avoid each station of life. Instead, maybe we would learn to get comfortable with discomfort and joyful when things are doubtful, for *it is often in the dark places that hope is born.*

Adversity in the grit of life creates a beautiful pearl of substance and a hope that is no longer easily shaken.

A Time to Worship

<u>Blessings by Laura Story</u> really sums up well how God can use our momentary problems and turn them around as blessings disguised.

Lord, thank You for changing our hope into one that never fades. Help us to trust you in the transitions of life that threaten to steal our hope and find ourselves filled with a reinvented hope, instead.

Day 15: Facing the Future

31 Days of Hope Reinvented

Inspirational Thought of the Day:
As we look through the ruins behind us, the past does not have to define us, but serves as a monument of what God brought us through.

Scripture of the Day:
Hebrews 11:1
"Now faith is confidence in what we hope for and assurance about what we do not see."

We have been facing a lot of difficult strongholds in the past couple weeks – fear, depression, disillusionment, judgment, sin, memories, reality and enemies. Some struggles we may have been aware of, some maybe not. The future on earth is a little more difficult to define, though. We cannot know it. At all. Such is the human condition. So how does one face the unknown? By faith.

Faith is the daughter of hope. We are confident not in faith itself, but solely in the object of our faith – our unchanging, faithful God.

The nebulous nature of what is to come can create in us a dependence on God or a shrinking back in fear, unsure of what God will allow across our path. This place of insecurity is beautiful, as it strips us of ourselves and brings us to our God, Who alone is our future.

Sometimes the past hurts so much that the future seems impossible. But, like the faith-filled saints who have gone before us in Hebrews 11, we can have a firm hope in the future because we know God's promises are yes and amen.

In the hall of fame of faith, we see saints of old who did not receive what was promised on this earth, but their faith in God led them to live sold-out to the promises of God. Sobered by life's often harsh realities, we learn that we cannot live for this world – it could never fully satisfy. This hope in what is to come is not for our lives to be perfect and not just for the promised reward. It is a hope that God will make every wrong right, that we will finally no longer be apart from Him and be in His presence. A hope that we will be like Him.

Let those words sink in. To be like Jesus. That is our chief goal in this life and God promises to fulfill it. Delivered from this earthly frame, there will be no more burden of sin. No more fear of man. No more tears, no more pain. What a hope this is!

As we look through the ruins behind us, the past does not have to define us, but serves as a monument of what God brought us through. As we seek to process the past and ready ourselves for the future, the lessons learned in all of our struggles and victories can prove invaluable. Nothing is wasted in God's hands and everything is redeemed for use in the future. Wow, what a hope. No longer do we have to fear what this life brings, for it is temporary and our hope is fixed on Christ alone!

A Time to Worship

<u>Blessed Be Your Name by Matt Redman</u> reminds us that whether God blesses or not, He can still be trusted to use it all for good.

Lord, thank You for a living hope that never fades – kept in Heaven by You. Help us to not lost sight of this hope. Give us a new hope that is only in You.

Day 16: Understanding Sin & The Sovereignty of God

31 Days of Hope Reinvented

Inspirational Thought of the Day:
God redeems our mistakes and uses them to fulfill His perfect purposes.

Scriptures of the Day:
Psalm 130:7
O Israel, hope in the Lord! For with the Lord there is steadfast love, and with him is plentiful redemption.

Romans 8:28 ESV
"And we know that for those who love God all things work together for good, for those who are called according to his purpose."

Ephesians 1:18
"I pray that the eyes of your heart may be enlightened in order that you may know the hope to which he has called you, the riches of his glorious inheritance in his holy people."

Sovereignty is a word that at once evokes comfort and fear simultaneously. We want to believe in a God Who is all-powerful and all-knowing, in complete control of everything.

We just aren't so comfortable with the fact that the other side of sovereignty sometimes means this awesome God also sovereignly allows suffering into our lives.

We tend to translate the truth of God's sovereignty into believing Christians will have a painless life – **if** they have enough faith. The mystery of God's sovereignty is much more complex than our simple definition of what is good or bad, though.

Enter mankind and his sins. How in the world is God sovereign over that?

As only our infinite God could, He weaves the reality of sin with His perfect plan and uses it all – for good. I know, we have all heard that verse many times, and frankly, it was not one of my favorite verses when I was smack dab in the middle of intense suffering. It was hard to see anything good that could possibly come from the mess I was in. But that was before I understood that my definition of good was skewed – in favor of me.

Dispensing with the perception that God's sovereignty means inactivity on His part or a fatalistic, apathetic view on our part, we still have to wrestle with the reality that God sovereignly allows suffering. But *without the pain we would not be grateful for the times when we do not have pain.*

If God knew ahead of time that we would sin, how is man to blame?

God's foreknowledge of our sins does not equate to culpability on His part. We cannot have it both ways. Either we have free will and are able to choose to sin or not, or God creates us to be robots with no will of our own.

Man's free will and God's overriding omniscience work in tandem and somehow amazingly God redeems our mistakes and uses them to fulfill His perfect purposes.

In the hands of God, He is able to take what was meant for evil and use it for good.

When our expectations for life are shattered, there is peace in resting in God's sovereignty. We are seen by a loving God. He will never forsake His children. He is All-Powerful and able to take our circumstances and turn them around. The patience, perseverance and beautiful character formed in the midst make it all worth it.

How about when other people's sin causes us pain? Why do we blame Him in the first place when sin and free will cause most of the messes we encounter? The same free will we want for ourselves we cannot take from others, even if they wrought pain in our lives. Can God restore our faith when it has been dashed to pieces? Can He use the death of dreams to bring new life?

Yes and Amen! Will the pain ever stop and the shame ever go away? Absolutely! But we might be surprised at how God uses the very thing we scorn. Like Paul who said he was "under great pressure far beyond his ability to endure…but this happened that we might not rely on ourselves but on God who raises the dead", we begin to understand that **we will be tested beyond our ability, but never beyond God's**. *His grace truly is sufficient. We just need to learn how to access it when the world is upside down.*

We can learn much from the Israelites. It was in their suffering that God made Himself available to them. When they were blessed before, they had forgotten God and were distracted with things of lesser value. Hardship had gotten their attention and had revealed to them that they were missing what mattered most – Knowing and enjoying God in this life that He gave.

For the Christian, there is hope in suffering because of our hope in God's sovereignty. He is faithful and He is a Redeemer of everything that transpires in our lives, all for His glory.

A Time to Worship

This song by Chris Tomlin says it well. Our God is Sovereign.

Lord, I stand in awe of You! I am so grateful that You are in complete control. Help us to surrender to Your sovereignty and trust in You always.

Day 17: The Christian Culture

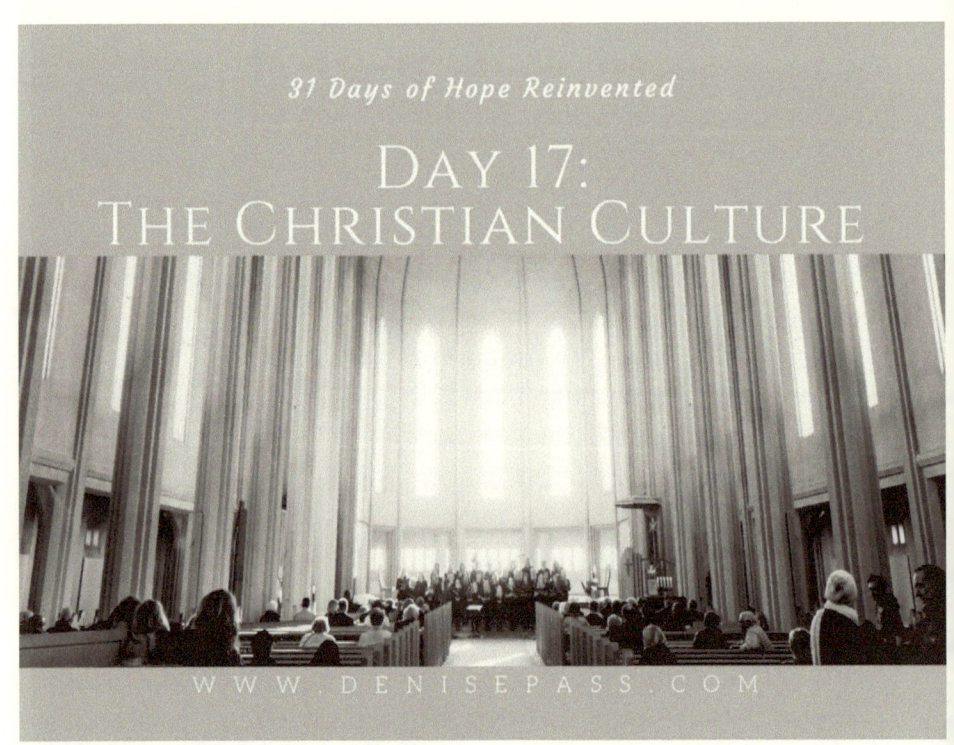

31 Days of Hope Reinvented

Inspirational Thought of the Day:
Our hope cannot be in people, or in a church. It has to be in Him alone.

Scriptures of the Day:
Philippians 2:19-21
19 I hope in the Lord Jesus to send Timothy to you soon, so that I too may be cheered by news of you. 20 For I have no one like him, who will be genuinely concerned for your welfare. 21 For they all seek their own interests, not those of Jesus Christ."

Hebrews 12:14-15
"Pursue peace with everyone, and holiness, for without it no one will see the Lord. 15 See to it that no one comes short of the grace of God, that no one be like a bitter root springing up and causing trouble, and through him many become defiled."

Sometimes our hope can be stolen from an unlikely place. Paul is not mincing words in this passage. To say that all the believers except Timothy sought after their own interests is astounding. Of course this is one verse of many and Paul often spoke with great encouragement about the believers he was working with.

Perhaps in this season in particular, he did not "feel the love" from the believers surrounding him.

I confess I have wanted to avoid this topic, but it has played such a big role in my healing as well as in my suffering. It is the elephant in the room that we want to avoid, but needs to be discussed in the hope of healing hearts who have been wounded by spiritual abuse or the Christian culture gone awry.

The first time I stepped into a church that was alive with joy and hope and fervent praise it felt like coming home. This is what it was all about – coming together and rejoicing in this new hope we had found. Church had been rather boring growing up – I did not know the LORD and we rarely went to church.

But then God saved me and I went to an amazing church, unlike any I had ever been to. There were exciting times serving in campus ministry, helping to start a church plant and serving on the worship team. Sweet, vibrant times of discipleship, fellowship and growing in the LORD.

When I was persecuted for my new faith, church was a refuge, the believers all surrounded me and it was family. Sometimes you wish you could bottle up the joy you have from one church experience and open it up from time to time when needed.

The church can serve as a great catalyst and cultivator of hope, but it can also serve as a place of great pain.

The pain is worsened by the fact that church is a place where we come for hope – a place where we know we are all accepted by Christ – but not necessarily by other Christians. When a Christian sins, it just hurts worse. It is not expected, but maybe it should be.

When we understand that the church is a place filled with sinful people, we clear up our disillusionment with the church. There is no perfect church and people sometimes can be prideful, selfish, legalistic, used as tools by the enemy.

Sometimes when life crushes our hope, we run to people or to the church as our refuge. This can be a source of inspiration, but it can also be a place of great stress and sorrow.

When my children and I were suffering greatly, we felt isolated and judged at church. The church simply did not know how to handle our situation. At the time it was very painful, but now I understand that they were just ill-equipped. Sometimes people meant well and sometimes they tried to manipulate us. When the church becomes a place of pain, it can hurt our faith. But God. Jesus brings healing and opens our eyes to realize that *our hope cannot be in people, or in a church. It has to be in Him alone.*

As we walk through life and encounter seasons that threaten to destroy us, we need to be in God's word foremost and to find like-minded believers who will stand with us. The people who caused us pain or judged us self-righteously – we can forgive them and realize they are misinformed and focused on earthly matters. Sometimes we, too, are small-minded and need grace.

The Holy Spirit can help us to get over our shock from snubbing, gossiping, jealousy, anger and rejection that come from believers. All of us are desperate for the grace of God and need to keep the main thing the main thing – being a beacon of hope to the world that desperately needs Jesus.

The church is not perfect, but the bride of Christ is indeed beautiful. Christ redeemed her and He will complete the work He has begun in her. Letting go of the judgments of man and embracing the acceptance we have in Christ offers a hope that never ends.

A Time to Worship

Stay where you are planted and help encourage the culture within your church to be one that pleases God. This song by Twila Paris is such a reminder of Who the church is. <u>How Beautiful.</u>

Lord, help us to keep our hope in You alone. Everything else disappoints, but You never do! Help your church to rise up and be loving and accepting, able to provide the hope You have given so abundantly.

31 Days of Hope Reinvented

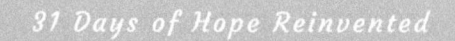

Day 18: Telling Ourselves the Truth – Exposing Our Unbelief

Inspirational Thought of the Day:
In the tunnels of life, we see one way out, but there are actually two. One path seeks God and the other seeks our own way.

Scripture of the Day:
Numbers 13:2, 17-20
13:2a "Send out men to investigate the land of Canaan, which I am giving to the Israelites. 17 When Moses sent them to investigate the land of Canaan, he told them, "Go up through the Negev, and then go up into the hill country 18 and see what the land is like, and whether the people who live in it are strong or weak, few or many, 19 and whether the land they live in is good or bad, and whether the cities they inhabit are like camps or fortified cities, 20 and whether the land is rich or poor, and whether or not there are forests in it. And be brave, and bring back some of the fruit of the land." **Now it was the time of year for the first ripe grapes.**

It is not until we are willing to examine ourselves and give our sin its worst name that we can begin to declare victory. Sin is deceitful, though, and we often do not recognize the subtleties of deception inherent in the walls of our mind.

Sometimes we can be convinced fully in our mind that we are "ok", but we are covering over this unsettled feeling that will not let go.
The irony in the discomforts of this life is that God is using them to deliver us from self-preoccupation and into a land of promise. Reminds me of those Israelites again.

There they were, on the edge of entering the promise land and God told them to go check it out. I wonder if he was delighting to see their joy at the blessings He had in store for them. Kind of like I get more excited than my kids to see their expressions as they see the good I have planned for them for various moments of celebration.

He sent them there when the land was full of hope – the grapes were ripe and plentiful, what a good Father. The scouts had a job to do and a choice to make. Would they focus on all the hope surrounding them, or the potential struggles? They told themselves lies. And they convinced others to believe them. God got pretty angry about it, too. Who wouldn't? Ever prepared an amazing surprise for someone only to have them say they don't like it?

Maybe in examining the lies they believed we might recognize our own self-deception, too.

Lie #1 – We are not able
Numbers 13:31 "We are not able to go up against these people, because they are stronger than we are".

Huge flaw in this calculation – kind of left out the God factor here. They gave a discouraging report that focused on their strength rather than God's and dissuaded the people from believing God.

Lie #2: Doubted God's goodness and intentions
Numbers 14:3 "Why has the LORD brought us into this land only to be killed by the sword, that our wives and our children should become plunder?"

Ouch. The first lie focused on our inability, but the second one accused God. To say that God just wanted to bring them out to kill them.

After all He had done for them. But our memories fade and we tend to forget all of the blessings when a massive thorn in our flesh comes knocking at our door.

Lie #3: Rebel against God and form our own plan.
Numbers 14:4 "So they said to one another, "Let's appoint a leader and return to Egypt."

The Israelites are in pretty bad shape to just say it is time to turn around and go home. Um, where was home? Living in slavery, eating onions and beaten all day? Sure sounds cozy.

They even dared to go ahead and try to claim the promised land their way – not God's. It did not turn out so well for them.
Lies will flood our mind unless we have the truth ready to dispute it. When we are tested like the Israelites were, we have to counter those attacks with the Word of God.

Truth #1: God is with us – do not fear
Numbers 14:9 "Only do not rebel against the Lord, and do not fear the people of the land, for they are bread for us. Their protection has turned aside from them, but the Lord is with us. Do not fear them!"

God demonstrated His presence over and over again, through His Word and through actions. We need to believe that He is with us and He is **for** us. It will be hard because reality sometimes hurts desperately. Maybe our hearts melt within us and it seems there is no way out – kind of like that tunnel image above. *Closed in by our circumstances, we see one way out, but there are actually two. One path seeks God and the other seeks our own way.*

Truth #2: Disbelief in God is hatred toward Him.
Numbers 14:11 "The Lord said to Moses, "How long will this people despise me, and how longwill they not believe in me, in spite of the signs that I have done among them?

Sometimes the fear of the LORD is a good reminder. When we see that our disbelief is wicked in God's sight, we need to repent and ask God for mercy, to give us faith. None of us would want to say we hate God. But disobedience is not love. If we love the Father, we will obey Him.

Truth #3: He is good and His plans are good.
Numbers 14:20 "Then the Lord said, 'I have forgiven them as you asked. 21 But truly, as I live, all the earth will be filled with the glory of the Lord.'"

Despite the constant disobedience of God's children, He still forgives and redeems. His plans will not be thwarted. He is loving, long suffering, kind.

Truth #4: He sees you.
Psalm 33:13-15 "The LORD watches from heaven; he sees all people. 14 From the place where he lives he looks carefully at all the earth's inhabitants. 15 He is the one who forms every human heart, and takes note of all their actions."

He rules over everything and still considers us. Wow. He saw the Israelites and He sees us. He knows our every thought and He chooses to love us, anyway. He saw me when I felt inadequate as a wife and sat motionless in the courtroom. He knew the plans that were ahead of me that I could not see when my life was a blur. When my body felt so weak from infirmity for years on end, He spoke strength, even if I could not feel it at the time. *Reality sometimes lies to us with its harsh expectations that are void of faith.*

The lies come in innocently enough, sometimes cloaked in righteous garb. But we do not have to fall victim to them. We are never trapped. God has a way out that will blow our mind and restore our hope in a way we never thought possible! *At the place of our devastation, there is always hope if we will just hold on and trust God.*

A Time to Worship

The *Voice of Truth by Casting Crowns* reminds us of the eternal view of all that happens in this life.

Lord, You are our ever present help in times of trouble. Help us to trust you.

Day 19: Fairy Tales Remixed

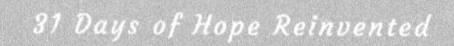

31 Days of Hope Reinvented

<u>Inspirational Thought of the Day</u>:
This life might not have a fairy tale ending on earth, but all of our sorrows will be swallowed up in Heaven and for all eternity.

<u>Scripture of the Day</u>:
John 10:28
"I give them eternal life, and they will never perish. No one can snatch them out of My hand."

Once upon a time (had to start this blog post like this, right?), ok, where was I? Oh yeah, once upon a time everything was perfect and a perfect looking person (who is the object of this story) suddenly had something imperfect thrust into her life. Whatever would she do? Oh, no worries, there is always a fairy something or another to help save the day after she goes through a significant amount of pain that makes it all worthwhile.

Sorry for the notable sarcasm present in that last paragraph. Fairy tales were not something I read to my kids much when they were little, and while I am at it, we did not celebrate Santa, either.

I know – I am a real killjoy. Or am I? I always wanted my kids to know that I told them the truth. Being fed lies can leave us hopeless and disillusioned when real life smacks you hard in the face. I wanted them to know that when I told them about Jesus that they could trust me, because I had laid a foundation of being a truth-teller.

Back to our story. We all somehow wish we could live in a fantasy world, because things always turn out well there. The "bad guys" always get what they deserve and the "good guys" always win out in the end. Life is good and it all revolves around us. Well, not really. In the story of our lives, a life well-lived revolves around Jesus, the real Hero of our story. He made us, and though He was God, He came in the form of man and laid down His own life for us. He did not seek a comfortable life nor man's praise. He, the God over all, **humbled** Himself! He did not complain about things being unfair, but entrusted Himself to His perfect Father, knowing the story would ultimately be for God's glory and His good.

Perhaps instead of craving a "perfect" life where we are surrounded by orchestral music constantly cheering us on in our adventures and where everyone adores us, we could have a change in our mentality. If we, too, laid down our lives as Christ did and sought to have Him live through us, then our perspective becomes one with a much different goal.

If my expectations are that all will work out well for me, my expectations can lead to idolatry. Ultimately, it ends well for those who are in Christ Jesus, but there will be times where life just does not make sense and sinful people seem to get away with wicked things. Other heroes of the faith got distracted with this reality, too, but they hoped in God.

When life hurts, we just want to escape. We want to hope in a perfect life. But maybe instead of that vain, temporary hope, we can begin to see a new hope forming.

Hope reinvented is a hope formed in the tragedies and mishaps of life. It is focused on hoping to live a life worthy of the life Christ gave on our behalf, no matter what circumstances are surrounding us.

> HOPE REINVENTED IS A HOPE FORMED IN THE TRAGEDIES AND MISHAPS OF LIFE. IT IS FOCUSED ON HOPING TO LIVE A LIFE WORTHY OF THE LIFE CHRIST GAVE ON OUR BEHALF, NO MATTER WHAT CIRCUMSTANCES ARE SURROUNDING US.
>
> WWW.DENISEPASS.COM

It is a passion to be faithful and to glorify God in the pains and the joys that life brings, a life that overcomes obstacles and looks to the Author of our faith instead of the obstacles themselves. That is my hope. I know it's hard to have faith when there is turmoil all around. It is a death, of sorts. But this life is not the end goal, anyway, and after death there is life.

This life might not have a fairy tale ending on earth, but all of our sorrows will be swallowed up in Heaven and for all eternity. We may not have a castle that eventually moth and rust destroy, but we have mansions in Heaven that never fade – beside the crystal lake, where we will have no more burdens and no more tears. Sounds better than any fairy tale ending I know – pretty amazing, in fact.

A Time to Worship

This song, _I Can Only Imagine_ by Mercy Me reminds us of the hope we have that never disappoints!

Lord, help our hope to be solely in living lives that glorify You. Take our burdens and use them to make us more like You!

Day 20: Uncovering the Goodness of God When Life Hurts

31 Days of Hope Reinvented

WWW.DENISEPASS.COM

Inspirational Thought of the Day:
We are often unaware of all the good God is accomplishing while we are surrounded by troubles.

Scriptures of the Day:
Hebrews 10:23
"Let us hold unswervingly to the hope we profess, for he who promised is faithful."

Romans 5:3-4
"Not only so, but we also glory in our sufferings, because we know that suffering produces perseverance; perseverance, character; and character, hope."

Psalm 119:68
"You are good, and do good."

In a barren wasteland covered in snow, we don't often think there is life underneath. All seems lifeless, suffocated by the layers of ice and snow. But when the "Son" rises and shines on all of creation, everything underneath the surface is exposed and brought to life.

I don't know where the errant theology slipped in that everything should be perfect in my life, but it did, almost unnoticed. I felt like I was owed a comfortable life because I was one of the King's daughters who ordered my life in a way to please God. Yep, if I am honest I really thought that. Subconsciously perhaps, but the expectations of my heart came to the surface.

It feels like a slap in the face when circumstances reach a painful climax that leaves us stunned and disillusioned. It was not what we were expecting.

Suddenly in a landscape we did not anticipate, we are lost. We manage to remember the faith we profess, but our deceitful hearts silently question why and sometimes start to cover over hurt that we don't dare expose.

In this crippled state, we feel engulfed by our emotions and the world feels blurry. Basic functioning is hard. But in the bittersweet place of brokenness there is a seed of hope that looks to our Creator. We want to believe Him, but we are afraid to have our "hopes" let down.

Confusion sets in as we try to understand what being "good" means when we consider the character of God. We live in a world that lives by the mantra, "you scratch my back and I will scratch yours". "You be nice to me", and vice versa. So when things happen that don't feel "nice", we cry "unfair". But let's consider what might be going on underneath the surface . . .

This God who allowed his people to be enslaved for 400 years also parted the sea and defeated their enemies. The slavery they bemoaned saved their lives from the famine in their own homeland. I am sure there were times when God's people saw this, but the burdens they bore distracted them and made them forget.

This same God who gave His people over to Babylon also restored them. He destroyed all living creatures on the face of the earth, but kept a remnant alive on the ark of every beast of the earth along with Noah and his crew.

So often we have no idea of all that God is doing behind the scenes. He is not surprised by our dilemma. He knew about it already and He wants to carry it for us. And maybe what we despise He actually has a divine purpose for allowing it in and it will ultimately bless us.

I don't know why Job had to suffer so much. I don't really get why satan was allowed to ask God to destroy poor Job. That's because so often we tend to think from our flesh. It does not make sense that any suffering at all could be defined as "good". Flesh cannot fully understand the ways of a Holy God.

Flipping our perspectives upside down, the Holy Spirit reveals what we really deserve and we accept the plan our Creator has for us. We belong to Him and He will heal all our pain and redeem it for His glory and our good.

The theme of discipline and redemption occurs many times in Scripture, and the discipline is not necessarily a lack of kindness. In His faithfulness, He disciplines those He loves. All hardship is to be endured as discipline by a loving Father. Discipline is a tough word. None of us like it if it is punitive.

We are often unaware of all the good God is accomplishing while we are surrounded by troubles. We wonder why we have to go through it all in the first place.

We do not have to be hypocritical and fake and pronounce when evil occurs in our lives that it is good. Of course it does not feel good. But in the Master's hands, what was meant for evil will be turned into good. That is just Who He is.

Have we lost someone we cared about? Have we suffered a horrific trial in our lives? In every pain, there is One Who identifies with us and chose to walk that path first. It will not be wasted.

Like Job, who said, "Though He slay me, I will trust in Him", may God help us to trust Him at all times. A goal for a perfect life void of pain is a shallow goal focused on self.

But when we consider that we were made for His pleasure, we find our greatest peace in surrendering to His plan even when it includes pain.

We hold firmly to God's hope because of the character behind His promise. He cannot be unfaithful. It is impossible for Him to do so.

A Time to Worship

Oh How He Loves Us So by David Crowder reminds us that God never removes His love from us. He is good. He is faithful. And you are loved eternally.

Lord, You are good all the time. Thank You for being our ever-present help in time of trouble.

Day 21: Hope's Debtor: Gratitude & Humility

31 Days of Hope Reinvented

Inspirational Thought of the Day:
This new reinvented hope longs to please God, not self.

Scripture of the Day:
Romans 5:3-4
"Not only so, but we also glory in our sufferings, because we know that suffering produces perseverance; perseverance, character; and character, hope."

This new reinvented hope is not formed without some friends – gratitude and humility. The beauty in the struggles of life is that they can work precious character into our hearts, if we let them.

Yielding requires trusting God in the face of suffering as well as in times of blessing. Gratitude is not a normal response in heartbreaking circumstances. In the fires of affliction, it is carefully molded through perseverance and a heart and mind change initiated by the Spirit of the living God.

Instead of having the attitude that we deserve what we want, we cry out and ask God to help us "put on" an attitude of gratitude.

Why did we think we deserved our way in the first place? The root of our expectations often exists in a self-centered hope. But this new reinvented hope – it longs to please God, not self. Only God can achieve that in man's heart.

Gratitude can't be mimicked. Anyone can be thankful in the moment, but an abiding gratitude stems from knowing God and having confidence that nothing ever transpires in our lives without His perfect good will. We can be truly grateful in sorrows because we know God wins in the end. Our hope is fixed on this truth and the fact that every jot and tittle, every moment of our lives – He is redeeming.

Humility cannot be manufactured by man, either. It comes in when we recognize, like Job, that when we question God, we truly do not understand Him or His ways. How can the one who is made know the mind of the Creator? And yet He draws us near to know Him. Humility is a death to our flesh that wants to reign. There is no greater example of humility than seeing our great Holy God choosing to bear our sins and suffer our punishment. And He did it with joy. Gratitude that souls could be won.

If we have the mindset of Christ, our trials become our triumphs and we see them through the scope of eternity. No more do we regret suffering. Instead we see ourselves as co-laborers with Christ and cry out for Him to use it to save just one.

Mankind does not want to take the blame for anyone else's actions. Our pride wells up and demands justice. Christ chose to be mistreated in the most extravagant demonstration of humble love ever seen.

A Time to Worship

Gratitude paves the way for healing. _Thank You_ by Hillsong is a great worship song that reminds us of all Christ has done.

Lord, help us to have Your understanding and to seek to honor You in every aspect of our lives. It is for Your glory alone that we live!

Day 22: Hope in Sorrows & Affliction

31 Days of Hope Reinvented

Inspirational Thought of the Day:
Our hope was always supposed to be in God Himself.

Scriptures of the Day:
Exodus 3:7
And Jehovah said, I have surely seen the affliction of My people who are in Egypt; I have heard their cry because of their taskmasters; for I know their sorrows.

2 Chronicles 33:12
"And when he was in affliction, he sought Jehovah his God, and humbled himself greatly before the God of his fathers."

Job 36:15
"He delivers the poor in his affliction, and opens their ears by oppression."

Psalms 119:50
"This is my comfort in my affliction; for Your Word has given me life."

Kneeling on the ground I looked up to the ceiling and cried out aloud. "Why, God?" "Why did I have to lose this child?" I reached for my Bible, asking God to help me understand.

I opened up to Psalm 119:67-72: "Before I was afflicted I went astray, but now I obey your word. 68 You are good, and what you do is good; teach me your decrees. ... 71 It was good for me to be afflicted so that I might learn your decrees. 72 the law from your mouth is more precious to me than thousands of pieces of silver and gold."

How could a miscarriage ever be good? But that day my tears were turned to joy as I was in awe of the truth that it was in love that God allowed affliction into my life. He is good and in His faithfulness He afflicts those he loves. How can it be faithful to allow affliction? Affliction works to deliver us from waywardness and causes us to draw nearer to God.

"Deep calls to deep". Going deeper with God often means finding him in a deep valley. God uses the greatest sorrows of our lives to heal us. We would never want to walk through deep waters of affliction, but it is affliction that accomplishes miracles within us and closeness with God we never knew before.

The hardest moments of my life have only caused me to go deeper with my God and I would not trade those precious gifts for the world. The hope in affliction is sure. The word says that God sees us in our suffering and He Himself will comfort us. There is no greater comfort than this.

It is affliction and sorrow that bring us to God. When we see how He cares for the lilies of the field and that a sparrow cannot fall to the ground apart from His will, we know that nothing happens to us apart from His sovereign good will and purposes.

The hope in affliction is different than the hope we had before the affliction. The hope for no suffering becomes a hope to glorify God in it. But more than that, we realize our hope for temporary gain pales in comparison to the hope that God has in store for us.

Our hope was never supposed to be in the hope the world offers. The world's hope ends. No, our hope was always supposed to be in God Himself.

"There is surely a future hope for you, and your hope will not be cut off." (Proverbs 23:18)

A Time to Worship

I wrote this song, _Deeper_ as part of our Seeing Deep EP. I pray that in whatever rejection or pain you have had to bear you will know the hope we have in affliction – we will go deeper with God and draw nearer to God!

Lord, You are our hope. Nothing else and on one else could ever be a living hope. Help us to abide in You always.

31 Days of Hope Reinvented

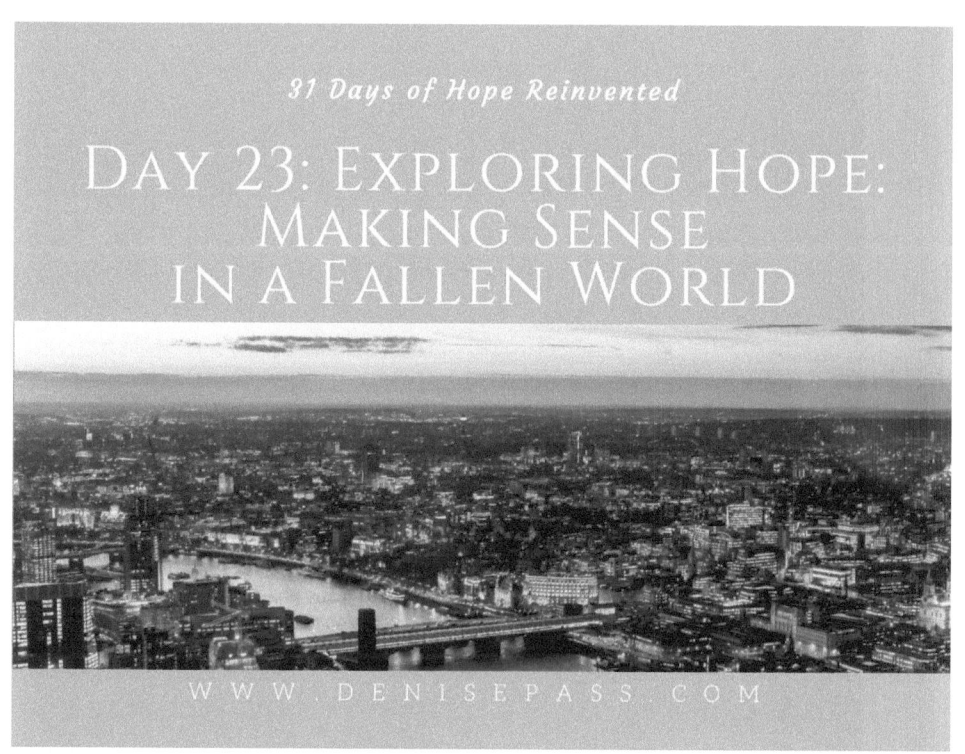

Day 23: Exploring Hope: Making Sense in a Fallen World

Inspirational Thought of the Day:
While the tragedies of this life do not make sense to our fleshly finite minds, God's word illumines our minds and hearts and helps us to see everything this life brings in light of eternity.

Scripture of the Day:
Ephesians 1:18-19
*18 "I pray that the eyes of your heart may be enlightened in order that you may **know the hope** to which he has called you, the riches of his glorious inheritance in his holy people, 19 and his incomparably great power for us who believe. That power is the same as the mighty strength."*

Living in a fallen world, we can get lost and become hopeless. There is no hope in a world without Christ, but in Christ we have discovered a new kind of hope.

As we have processed our grief and sought to understand the heart of God in our struggles, we come to a place where we apply this new hope in this broken place we live.

Looking over the rugged landscape ahead of us, we learn to apply all that we have learned as we have sought to not just restore our hope, but have a living lasting hope.

Our Compass. At the core of this new reinvented hope is viewing the world through a biblical lens. The old default method of letting feelings and thoughts rule our mind is taken captive and we search the word of God for guidance in the bumps and blessings we encounter. While the tragedies of this life do not make sense to our fleshly finite minds, God's word illumines our minds and hearts and helps us to see everything this life brings in light of eternity.

Trust. Proverbs 3:5-6 says it well – "Trust in the LORD with all your heart, and do not rely on your own understanding. 6 Acknowledge him in all your ways, and he will make your paths straight." This new hope cannot be based on our own understanding. When we trust the LORD with moments of life that don't make sense, we experience an abundant joy and a peace that the world can never remove. He is trustworthy.

Expectations. The expectation of the righteous is joy, but that does not mean a problem-free life. "There is surely a future hope for you, and your hope will not be cut off." (Proverbs 23:8). Our new reinvented hope never ends. Breathe that truth in. It is not based in this earth, nor in anyone or anything but God alone and He has no beginning or end.

A Time to Worship

The song, *Forever* by Kari Jobe reminds us that God's purposes will stand forever. The temporary problems in this world will all be swallowed up by God's ultimate victory.

Lord, thank you for providing a hope that is secure and lasts forever.

Day 24: Superficial Hope

31 Days of Hope Reinvented

Inspirational Thought of the Day:
We have to let go of our hope to find it.

Scripture of the Day:
1 Corinthians 15:19
"If in Christ we have hope in this life only, we are of all people most to be pitied."

Hope is vain if it is in the wrong place. Worse yet, pretending to hope but inwardly doubting really can leave us bewildered and disillusioned. Hope is a scary thing. *We have to let go of our hope to find it.* Sounds ironic, I know. But the hope we cultivated in the natural cannot compare with the new hope we have found which is not based on human principles.

We cannot walk on the fence of pretending to have this new Reinvented Hope while trying to maintain our former hope. Often times people remain hopeless because they don't dare to hope again due to the fear of their hopes getting crushed.

But *this new Reinvented Hope cannot be crushed – it is eternal.* It is not based on anything temporary or of this world, but in Christ alone. It is *not superficial, but supernatural.*

Rising above the fear of unfulfilled hopes, this new Reinvented Hope cannot be manufactured or faked – but it can be formed in the deep chasms of life in the word of God.

A Time to Worship

On the horizons of our lives, there is a hope ahead that never fades, discovered in the pages of Scripture and in the surrender of our hearts. This worship song from Jeremy Camp called, *There Will Be a Day* says it well. He is the hope we long for!

Lord, thank You for showing me this new hope in You. Through all of the grief process when I was dismayed that my hope could never look the same, You showed me I never would want it to. Your hope is enough for me.

Day 25: The Promise of Hope

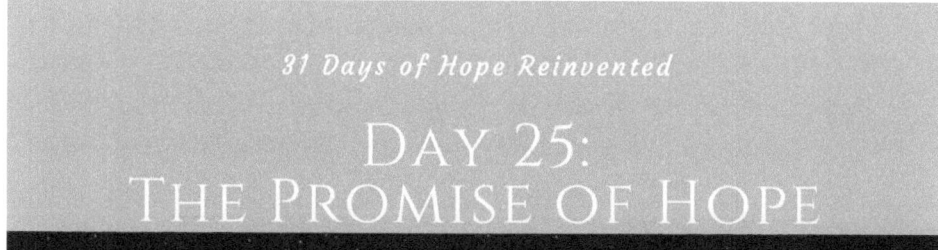

31 Days of Hope Reinvented

Inspirational Thought of the Day:
Keep it simple like Abe. Hope in God alone.

Scripture of the Day:
Psalm 71:14
"But as for me, I will always have hope; I will praise you more and more."

"The LORD took him outside and said, 'Gaze into the sky and count the stars–if you are able to count them!' Then he said to him, 'So will your descendants be.'"

What a picture of our Father, delighting in revealing the hope He had for Abraham. In that moment, standing next to the Creator of all that surrounded Him, Abe must have been overwhelmed at such a statement. His descendants would be more than he could count? He wanted to hope that he would have descendants, did he dare to?

Barren and childless, Abraham believed God and the hope He promised and it was reconciled to Him as righteousness.

He did not get caught up in his circumstances or the very raw reality that his wife and he were old, beyond the years of procreation and, well, childless. Abraham was 75 years old when God first called him to leave his country. He was 90 when God renewed His promise to him. It would be another ten years later, at age 100, that Abraham and Sarah finally had their son.

25 years. In our instant society, hope would be all but dysfunctional and destroyed if we were told a promise and God took 25 years to have it come true. We are prone to doubt, but there is such an amazing example in Abraham's simple belief. "God said it, I believe it, that settles it."

When we seek just to find hope, we miss out on the relationship with God. When we seek God, we find Him and discover a hope unending.

The promise in a Reinvented Hope is that the One Who made the promise is always faithful to keep every single promise He has ever made. God cannot fail in delivering on the hope He offers. It might take a little while for the promises to unfold, but the One Who spoke them rules over everything and surely will bring it about. Keep it simple like Abe. Hope in God alone.

The hope of wanting things for ourselves or this earth cannot compare with a hope in Christ that ultimately never will disappoint. Earthly hopes fade away. But God's hope is built on His promises – it simply is and always has been.

A Time to Worship

The worship song, <u>*Everlasting God*</u> *by Lincoln Brewster* is such an encouragement when we contemplate how to cultivate our hope and strength - by waiting on the LORD.

Lord, Your promises are sure. You are faithful and true! Thank You that we are people of hope and of Your promise.

Day 26: The Foundation of Hope

31 Days of Hope Reinvented

Inspirational Thought of the Day:
The battle for *Hope Reinvented* begins at the foundation of our hope and is a battle in the mind.

Scripture of the Day:
Romans 15:4
"For everything that was written in former times was written for our instruction, so that through endurance and through encouragement of the scriptures we may have hope."

Ephesians 2:12
"In those days you were living apart from Christ. You were excluded from citizenship among the people of Israel, and you did not know the covenant promises God had made to them. You lived in this world without God and without hope."

1 Corinthians 3:11
"For no one can lay any foundation other than the one already laid, which is Jesus Christ."

When we are at the place of broken dreams, trying to rebuild our hope can seem futile, especially when the future ahead does not appear to have hope in the natural.

If you have been reading this series on *Hope Reinvented*, we have walked through all of the pitfalls and detractors from having a living hope in Christ. We have examined our former hope and let it go if it was not the hope God has for us. We have also seen that real hope is only found in Christ. Now we will examine what is at the foundation of this Hope Reinvented in Christ alone.

God's Word. At the foundation of this *Reinvented Hope* is God's Word. Man's word or promise could never fulfill the demands of a hope that never fails. His promises speak life when death is all we see, but another friend at the level of foundation must be present to apply God's word ...

Trust. *Trusting when everything is going well is not trust at all.* But trusting when nothing is going well – now this is trust. Some people think it is foolish to trust in what you cannot see, but this is the definition of faith, as well. Without faith no one can please God. God delights in us and in giving us His promises. He loves it when we look to Him and hope in Him. There is another layer of the foundation of hope – relationship.

Relationship is a necessary layer in our foundation, for without it we cannot claim the promises given by God. Sometimes we can be guilty of just wanting relief from the burdens of this life and seeking the hope of God to escape. Having a relationship with God enables us in times of adversity and also becomes our beacon of hope as we have confidence in the promises He has made to those who trust Him.

Action. As we begin to live out this *Reinvented Hope* we see another layer in our foundation – action. *Living hope in action means we live boldly in the face of dashed hopes.* We exemplify this reality by going against the flesh and taking God's promises at face value.

Studying His Word, applying it, memorizing it and living it out is what makes this eternal hope come to life. Action must accompany mentally agreeing with God's hope.

Discipline. Consistency in nurturing our hope is necessary to cultivate and grow our confidence in this secure hope we have. Taking captive hopeless thoughts and replacing them with God's, coupled with studying His word daily are not optional. We will be tossed to and fro, otherwise.

When my world was encompassed by constant strife (and this still happens from time to time), I thirsted for God's promises and read them constantly. I put myself in a place to receive those promises by seeking Him fervently and crying out for Him to deliver me instead of running to other vices or "hopes". The challenge in such times is to not look around you at the waves or the supposed failures. They work to tear down our hope.

Mental toughness is created and our faith strengthened when we choose to focus only on God and His Word. *Sometimes we have to guard our heart to keep away the "hope stealers".* These hope stealers or crushers can be pretty convincing, but they are not eternal.

The battle for Hope Reinvented begins at the foundation of our hope and is a battle in the mind. We must choose which hope we believe in and fight for it with all we have. I close today with words from Woodrow Kroll from his series, "Back to the Bible": "No one who utterly despairs will pray, for prayer is the proof of lingering hope. Even in the midst of despair, the psalmist recognizes that, should there be any hope, it will be found only in God."

A Time to Worship

Our hope is firmly on our living God. Sing <u>*Hosanna*</u> by Hillsong - our Lord is coming again!

Lord, You are awesome and faithful, our only Hope! Help us to stay rooted in this hope and to share this hope as stewards of the only real eternal hope that only You can give.

Day 27: The Formation of Hope

31 Days of Hope Reinvented

Inspirational Thought of the Day:
Our hope is formed as we delight in God as our life.

Scripture of the Day:
Lamentations 3:24
"The Lord is my portion," says my soul, "therefore I will hope in him."

Romans 15:13
"May the God of hope fill you with all joy and peace as you trust in Him, so that you may overflow with hope by the power of the Holy Spirit."

Hope is often formed in an interesting place. It begins possibly with devastating circumstances that rip away the former hope we had and leave us in a stupor. In this vacuum, there is a holy wrestling that causes us to examine what hope we ever really had.

As the foundation for *Reinvented Hope* is being laid, we are forming the prospects of this new hope we have found. We no longer have security in anything else but God.

Our God of hope causes us to overflow with His hope, joy and peace as we trust in Him.

Our hope is formed as we delight in God as our life. At first it can be a little shaky testing out this new hope as it is being formed. We might take a step and look at circumstances and doubt whether the hope can truly hold us up when life's challenges overcome us. This is where we learn to trust God. Moment by moment, looking to Him instead of our former way of looking to solutions within ourselves or other people.

Much like a potter removes that which distracts from the beauty and capability of the object he is forming, God will remove what we have been formerly trusting in and replace it with Himself. When we have nothing else to hope in, we find our hopes formed and fulfilled in Christ alone.

A Time to Worship

The song, *The Potter's Hand* by Hillsong speaks of our God drawing us and molding us to be more like Him. What a hope!

Lord, You are our hope! Mold us to be like You and make our dreams into Yours.

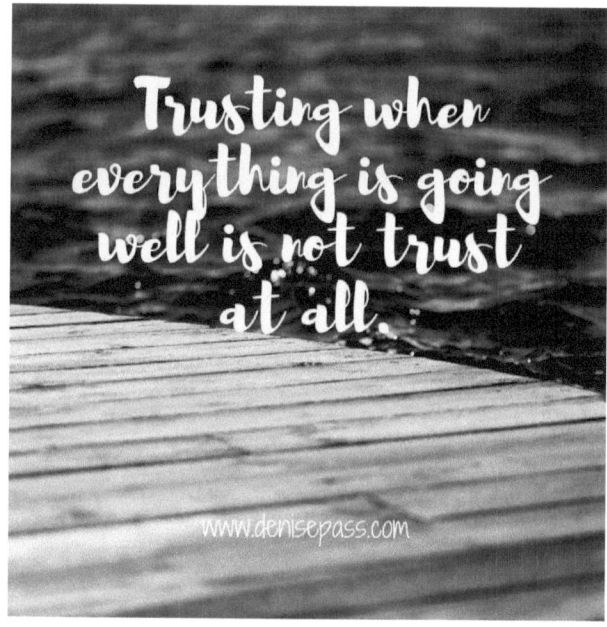

Day 28: The Fruition of Hope

31 Days of Hope Reinvented

Inspirational Thought of the Day:
Having our hope transfixed on God causes us to seek to do His mission instead of our own.

Scriptures of the Day:
Colossians 1:27
"To them God has chosen to make known among the Gentiles the glorious riches of this mystery, which is Christ in you, the hope of glory."

Romans 5:5
"And hope does not put us to shame, because God's love has been poured out into our hearts through the Holy Spirit, who has been given to us."

Here we are – we have come so far. What began as a seemingly hopeless situation has been transformed into a Hope Reinvented and the fruit of this new hope we have found is sweet, indeed.

When life disrupts the plans we have, it is an opportunity to trust God and see what He accomplishes as we hope in Him. With this new hope there is no more shame, no more cause to wonder if God is for us.

We are confident of God's purposes even when the situation is bleak. This is the fruit of a life invested in God's hope for us instead of our own. Bearing within us God's perfect peace and love, His hope brings our hearts in sync with God's purposes as we look to Him as our hope.

When I sat in the back of a police station for the second time due to yet another court error, the pain of the nonsensical mess I was in wrecked my heart and hurt my faith. Why would God allow this? But the LORD used the painful mishaps of life and the relentless pursuit from others against me to cause me to desperately draw nearer to Him.

I longed for a simple life again, but realized that this hope would keep me in a state of comfort and complacency. It felt like walking on water as I stepped out the boat of my hopes and placed all my dreams in His Holy hands. This hew hope was unending and filled my heart with joy and laughter, even as my old hope faded away.

When a person has a living hope, the resulting fruit is a life lived for God's glory instead of for vain hopes. *Having our hope transfixed on God causes us to seek to do His mission instead of our own.*

A Time to Worship

The fruit of hope is founded in placing our belief and trust in One alone - God. Let's sing, <u>*We Believe*</u> by the News Boys.

Thank You, LORD, for fixing our eyes on You – the Author and completer of our faith. Hope in You is always well placed and fulfills our life purpose.

Day 29: Hope Discovered

31 Days of Hope Reinvented

Inspirational Thought of the Day:
Those who "catch" this Reinvented Hope are on the hunt for it.

Scriptures of the Day:
Psalm 31:24
"Be strong and take heart, all you who hope in the Lord."

Hebrews 10:23
"Let us hold unswervingly to the hope we profess, for he who promised is faithful."

Psalm 130:5
"I wait for the Lord, my whole being waits, and in his word I put my hope."

We are nearing the end of our journey exploring this new Hope Reinvented, which was found as we applied God's precious word and promises through all the obstacles life has thrown at us.

Discovering this hope was not easy, but we can say that it was worth it no matter what the cost – to gain this precious gift of a hope everlasting.

As we run this race and explore this life to see what our hope really is, we first have examined what it is not.

- Reinvented hope is not in belongings or riches.
- Reinvented hope is not in having a perfect life.
- Reinvented hope is not in any person or thing.
- Reinvented hope is not in any achievements I pursue or gain.
- Reinvented hope is not in the avoidance of pain.
- Reinvented hope is not in another man's praise or acceptance.

Oddly enough, Reinvented hope is discovered when:

- Rejection comes knocking on our door, causing us to run to our Father for lasting acceptance.
- Illness comes, bringing suffering that humbles us and causes us to look for a hope beyond our pain.
- Sorrow knocks on our door unexpectedly, jolting us into the reality that our hopes are no more.
- When the pressures of this life build to an intense level – finances or relationships in turmoil – and cause us to find resolution.

It is in these desperate moments of life that we look up to our God and need something more. Aware that this life has not delivered what we had hoped, we come before God bankrupt with scarcely a hope at all.

We battle through disillusionment and fight to finally obtain an authentic definition of what it means to walk side-by-side with our Creator and really place our hope and trust in Him.

I believe *those who "catch" this hope are on the hunt for it*. They don't leave the race of this life, despite many discouraging "hope killers". They are instead thrusting themselves forward with whatever strength they have left, and placing themselves in the mercies of God.

I am not much of a runner, but I run anyway. I have had to battle numerous autoimmune diseases and have many more days with pain than without. Pain has a way of making things feel impossible. Hope seems futile when just basic functioning is a challenge.

In the midst of some of my greatest pain, I have written love notes to my God that could not have been written had I not been brought to my knees. As I surrendered to the adjustments I had to make to be able to still be productive, a funny thing happened. I was surprised by gratitude and discovered a hope that was greater than when I had been well and I worshiped God in a way I had not before.

I still have to guard my health, but in His mercy God has placed many of my autoimmune diseases underneath my feet in remission. What a good God. But the lessons learned are even more precious to me than the healing He has brought. I will praise my God whether I am well or not, for in all of it, He is my hope and He will use it all for my good and His glory.

When we discover this hope, we need to be like the Psalmist and hold onto this Hope Reinvented with all our being. The storms of life ebb and flow, but God's hope is constant throughout. As we wait for our ultimate redemption, His hope and His word are our strength and enablement to live a worthy life full of hope for His glory.

A Time to Worship

<u>You Are Worthy</u> is a song I wrote about the worth of our God, which far surpasses anything this world promises . As we focus on God's worth and character, our problems become smaller, we discover lasting hope and joy and are lost in worship of Him.

Oh God, I am overcome by Your goodness! Thank You for revealing this awesome hope we have in You! Help us to rely on You and not anything You created. Open our eyes when we are tempted to look to anything else other than You for our salvation.

Day 30: Hope Reinvented

31 Days of Hope Reinvented

Inspirational Thought of the Day:
God wants to take us to a higher place that far surpasses simply hoping for status quo.

Scriptures of the Day:
1 Corinthians 13:13
"And now these three remain: faith, hope and love. But the greatest of these is love."

Romans 8:24-25
"But For in this hope we were saved. Now hope that is seen is not hope. For who hopes for what he sees? But if we hope for what we do not yet have, we wait for it patiently."

Well here we are. We've arrived. Well, not really. Reinvented Hope requires maintenance, but "hope"fully as we've examined the hope we have, we've exposed areas in our lives where our hope was in the wrong place and refocused our hope in the right place – Jesus alone.

We began this quest for Hope Reinvented with the understanding that to be human is to hope – to hope and believe in an ultimate good end.

God uniquely made us with a craving for hope and something more than we see around us. *This is not ingratitude, but a longing placed there by a sovereign God, who knew we needed to be people of Hope to live worthy lives.*

God wants to take us to a higher place that far surpasses simply hoping for status quo, the avoidance of pain or even temporary success in this world. As we have walked through the maze of this life we have learned to navigate disillusionment and suffering by looking up over the walls of doubt that threaten to block our view of God's hope.

Sometimes our troubles actually give birth to hope and help us to understand our hope was very different from what we thought we needed in the first place. As we walk through many troubled times that we never thought would be a part of our testimony, we learn to trust in our God and see that the sweetness of surrendering to His sovereignty is unparalleled with any other solution this world has to offer.

Our solace in suffering is that our Savior willingly chose the road of suffering that we wanted to deny and is able to guide us on that path and give us victory in surrendering to His hope.

Hope Reinvented is not dependent on anything this world offers. The quest for this eternal hope causes us to lift our eyes to the hills and see where our hope comes from – God and His word.

A Time to Worship

Our lives are not about us, after all. <u>*All About You*</u> is a song I wrote that reminds us that everything in our lives is about His glory - not ours.

Lord, thank You for being our hope. Help us to never forget the hope we have learned and to share this living hope with others, too.

31 Days of Hope Reinvented

Day 31: Hope Reinvented

WWW.DENISEPASS.COM

Inspirational Thought of the Day:
Hope Reinvented survives in the harshest of environments and is an anchor, sure and steady.

Scriptures of the Day:
Hebrews 6:19
"We have this as a sure and steadfast anchor of the soul, a hope that enters into the inner place behind the curtain..."

1 Peter 3:15
"But in your hearts revere Christ as Lord. Always be prepared to give an answer to everyone who asks you to give the reason for the hope that you have. But do this with gentleness and respect."

Zechariah 9:12
"Return to your stronghold, O prisoners of hope; today I declare that I will restore to you double."

Psalm 119:114
"You are my hiding place and my shield; I hope in your word."

You made it! Sifting through our hopes and dreams, fulfilled, broken or unrealized, has taken us on a voyage to discover a hope we never thought was possible.

Hope Reinvented survives in the harshest of environments and is an anchor, sure and steady. It reminds us of our core purpose in this life – to glorify God and live a worthy life filled with His eternal hope – and beckons us back to our Creator and His vision for this precious life He has given.

As you have assessed where your hope lies, have you had a change of perspective in hope? Was it all you "hoped it would be"? (Sorry, my corny sense of humor had to chime in there).

If you are in a place of brokenness, hope is not easily seen. How have you navigated through such times?

This knowledge of the hope God has for us cannot be kept a secret. People need to know this life was never meant to be lived for the here and now alone. There is hope when life is not hopeful, but it is not in things or positions or earthly temporary success. Hope Reinvented is found in His precious Word alone as we are in a relationship with the God of this universe, our Abba Father.

Thank you for taking this time to come with me and explore what Hope Reinvented looks like. God makes all things new and His hope for you is sure.

A Time to Worship

Song of Hope by the Robbie Seay band is an appropriate ending to this devotional. Let's worship Him, our Living Hope!

Oh God, You are our portion, our delight! Thank You that You have not left us without hope. We worship You, our Eternal Hope!

About the Author

Currently the Worship Leader for New Life Community Church in Louisa, VA, Denise writes, sings, and proclaims God's goodness based on her real life experiences. A published author with The Upper Room, she blogs devotional thoughts and also ghost writes. Denise's debut album, "Just Fine", released in 2002, and launched her music and speaking ministry in the Mid-Atlantic states.

Denise's next album, "Praying For You" (2005) had a track "Reign in Me" that received airplay in 11 states. This CD received Album of the Year from the Independent Gospel Music Association.

In 2007 she was awarded first place in the pop/contemporary music category by the President of K-LOVE radio in partnership with the International Music Ministry Association.

At the end of 2007, within months of receiving this recognition, Denise's life was suddenly upended by a personal crisis that tore at the very fabric of her family. A home-school mom of 5 children, Denise navigated through intense personal trials which have now formed a platform of Reinvented Hope and passionate worship.

RESOURCES

Seeing Deep

Sure, the ministry name is grammatically incorrect, but the purposes are true north.

Christian CCM artist Denise Pass delivers a powerful authentic message through song and word, spoken and written underneath the ministry umbrella "Seeing Deep". With a goal of discipleship and authentic faith, Seeing Deep seeks to be a compass grounded in Scripture and a place where real problems meet real, transparent faith and needed answers in Scripture.

The Word of God is relevant to all of life's problems. Sometimes we just get lost and confused in the many crises of life. The Seeing Deep blog is a practical blog applying biblical solutions to the relativistic philosophies of our day.

Denise's inspirational, worship and contemporary Christian music is a place of healing in life's storms. Denise's music is currently on radio, including a new song, "You are Worthy", produced in Ed Cash's studio and released in January 2017 to radio.

Currently working on a Worship project that will correlate with the "Hope Reinvented" project, Denise is available to speak at women's conferences, lead worship for your special event, retreat or conference, or serve as a guest artist in concert.

For booking requests, contact Denise at:

booking@denisepass.com
www.denisepass.com

(C) 2016 Denise Pass. All rights reserved.

www.denisepass.com

Questions? Comments?

Visit Denise's website and leave feedback. We'd love to hear from you!